As one of the world's longest established
and best-known travel brands
Thomas Cook are the experts

For more than 135 y
guidebooks have unlocked th
of destinations around th
sharing with travellers a w
experience and a passion for travel.

Rely on Thomas Cook as your travelling companion on your next trip and benefit from our unique heritage.

Thomas Cook **traveller** guides

NAPLES & THE AMALFI COAST

Ryan Levitt

Written by Ryan Levitt, updated by Jo-Ann Titmarsh
Original photography by Conor Caffrey

Published by Thomas Cook Publishing
A division of Thomas Cook Tour Operations Limited.
Company registration no. 3772199 England
The Thomas Cook Business Park, 9 Coningsby Road
Peterborough PE3 8SB, United Kingdom
Email: books@thomascook.com, Tel: + 44 (0) 1733 416477
www.thomascookpublishing.com

Produced by Cambridge Publishing Management Limited
Burr Elm Court, Main Street, Caldecote CB23 7NU

ISBN: 978-1-84848-224-1

Series Editor: Maisie Fitzpatrick
Production/DTP: Steven Collins

Printed and bound in Italy by Printer Trento

Cover photography: © Pictures Colour Library

Contents

Introduction

Conquered throughout the ages by numerous counts and courts, the city of Naples combines influences from dozens of regions across the European continent. Spanish architecture, Baroque splendour, Italian flair and the Arabian kasbah come together in this city overlooked and often overshadowed by Mount Vesuvius – the volcano that gives the region both its incredibly fertile soil and its somewhat threatening reputation.

The Neapolitan spirit is one that Anglo-Saxons often find difficult to comprehend. Whether arriving by plane, train or boat, the sight of Naples' choking traffic, crumbling masonry and the frequent arm-flailing and dramatic street-side arguments among its charismatic citizens may make you wonder why you ever decided to book a holiday here. Don't take this fear of the foreign as a sign to flee to Capri, Ischia or any of the more salubrious locales dotted in and around the Bay of Naples – rather, take the time to scratch the dusty and rubbish-strewn streets to discover this city brimming with culture, incredible gourmet delights, secret palazzo hideaways, labyrinthine alleyways and a sense of excitement unsurpassed anywhere else in Italy.

This chaotic atmosphere owes much to the area's talent for survival. Naples has faced destruction in the eye on more than just a few occasions, whether it be due to wartime bombings, aching poverty or natural disasters. But its future is looking up. A Neapolitan revival has been brewing for over a decade, ever since the city hosted the G7 meeting of economic superpowers back in 1994. As part of the clean-up campaign tied in with the city's summit duties, new metro stations were built, the national *Mani Pulite* (clean hands) campaign was launched to reduce corruption, and city streets and roadways were brightened up to showcase the city and its Renaissance to the world. Poverty and crime may still exist, but the likelihood of foreigners being on the receiving end of theft and muggings is exceedingly slim – as long as you don't go around flashing your new Rolex to the masses.

While the city continues to be one of the most cash-strapped in the nation, it can still put on a good show. Opera performances at Teatro di San Carlo – Italy's oldest theatre – are reputed to be second only to Milan's La Scala.

The art collections at the Museo di Capodimonte are packed with examples of the masters from the 16th to the 19th centuries, and the treasures of Pompeii are brilliantly illuminated in the massive Museo Nazionale Archeologico. If you time it right, you may even be able to catch one of the temporary exhibitions of cutting-edge modern art at the Castel Sant'Elmo. And that's not even including the painstakingly excavated ruins of Pompeii and Herculaneum, the trappings of the island playgrounds of the rich – Capri and Ischia – or the jaw-dropping views and cliff-side towns that dot the Amalfi Coast.

So pour yourself a glass of *limoncello*, find yourself a cosy view of the bay and prepare yourself for an unforgettable experience enjoyed by millions of tourists since the days when a few ancient Greek explorers decided that this corner of the Med would make a nice place to live. You may be branded a *straniero* (foreigner), but you're sure to be given a welcome that will make you feel right at home.

The Naples of today

The city

At 40.8 degrees north, 14.4 degrees east, the city of Naples is the third-largest city in Italy (after Milan and Rome), and is situated directly on the Bay of Naples, which stretches from the port town of Pozzuoli in the north to the sweeping Sorrento Peninsula in the south. Just over 40km (25 miles) separates the two corners of the bay as the crow flies. Naples is approximately one-third of the way down the coastline from Pozzuoli on the way to Sorrento and the Amalfi Coast.

Naples proper boasts a population of approximately one million. Including the suburbs, this number increases to three million inhabitants dwelling in geographic locations as diverse as the fertile Campania plain and the high grounds, craters and hills formed by ancient volcanoes. Most of the commutable population is linked by train services that plod their way alongside the Bay of Naples coastline at frequent intervals throughout the day.

The islands of Capri, Ischia and Procida are located just off the Campanian coast. Ferries link the islands to each other and to the port towns of Pozzuoli, Sorrento, Positano and Naples. Ferry rides between the islands and Naples take approximately an hour and fifteen minutes. Less time is required if you catch one of the frequent rapid hydrofoils.

Climate

Naples boasts a Mediterranean climate that ranges in heat from up to 40°C (104°F) in the height of summer down to 0°C (32°F) in December and January. During the peak months of July and August, temperatures in the city can be sweltering, with extremely high humidity levels doing little to alleviate the heat. The islands of Capri, Ischia and Procida experience cooling sea breezes during this period, yet also become packed with tourists, thus making any climatic benefits minimal when combined with the volume of humanity flocking to their sun-kissed shores.

Spring and autumn are often the best times to visit, when limited tourist numbers and invariably warm temperatures show Naples at its best. Hotel bookings tend to be down during this shoulder season, which often affords optimum weather conditions and better options for a tight budget. March, April and September occasionally experience heavy showers, but they quickly disappear to leave the city bathed in crystal-clear air and cleaner, washed-down streets. The post-shower period is the perfect time to search for higher ground and capture city panoramas when Naples is bathed in a golden glow.

Between November and February, the air becomes clear and cold, rarely dropping below freezing. The winter months often dust snow on the top of Vesuvius, giving it an alpine resort look. While you run the risk of dreary, wet weather during the colder months, the periods of drizzle and cloud invariably leave within a couple of days to reveal spectacularly clear views.

The areas of Naples

The geography of the city is largely determined by the hills and coastline carved by the ancient volcanic activity of the area. While the Centro Storico is the heart of Naples, it is by no means the only district worth exploring. The oldest part of the city, its streets are maze-like, twisting and turning according to the needs of merchants and residents of times gone by. Disasters, destruction and subsequent unregulated rebuilding have done much to complete the seemingly chaotic mess of Neapolitan traffic. The ancient Greeks attempted to impose order on the place with a grid pattern of streets in central Naples, but development throughout the ages has largely obliterated this original attempt at order. The Port and University district is predominantly an industrial

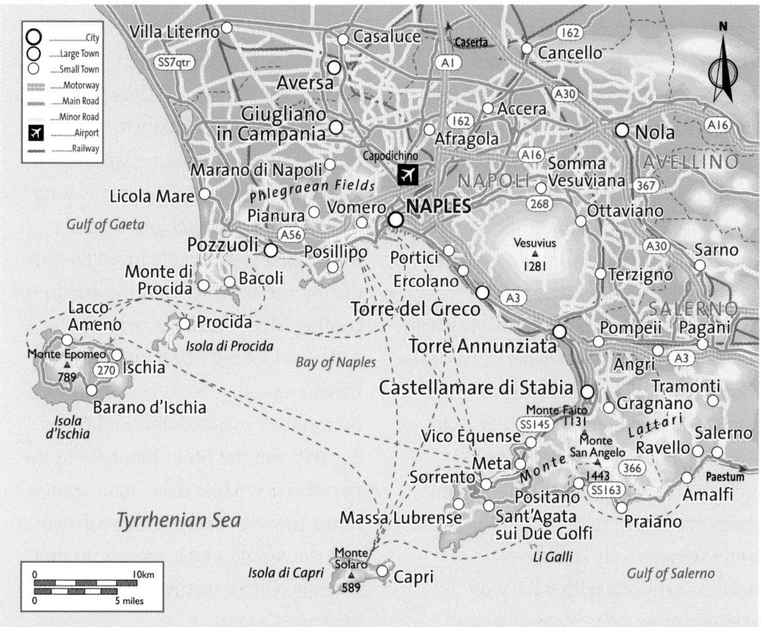

wasteland. Attempts are being made to clean up the area in order to revitalise the community and remove a few of the more distracting and polluting sights, but the bureaucracy and poverty of the city have made project development slow to come to fruition. A new metro line linking this neighbourhood to the rest of the city is set to open by the end of 2011, which should do much to help alleviate the choking traffic. This area lies due south of the Centro Storico directly on the waters of the Bay of Naples. The Via Duomo bisects both neighbourhoods almost directly down the middle and acts as a convenient road to traverse between the two communities.

Royal Naples, situated west of the main port, holds the bulk of the treasures of Naples' regal past, including the Palazzo Reale and the Castel dell'Ovo. Noted more for its shopping and archaeological treasures is the Quartieri Spagnoli, almost directly north of the Royal Naples quarter. To reach the Quartieri Spagnoli, follow the sound of ringing cash registers up the Via Toledo towards the Museo Nazionale Archeologico (Archaeological Museum). If you enter Sanità (anywhere east of the Museo Nazionale Archeologico) then you've gone too far. The lack of chain stores should be your first clue.

Two hills sandwich the city against the port – Vomero and Capodimonte. Both are relatively middle-class neighbourhoods with a bevy of attractions to draw in the masses. Luxury hotel options line the Corso Vittorio Emanuele in Vomero, with the Castel Sant'Elmo providing excellent views of the city below. Vomero is also where you will find the funiculars for which the city is famous. Via Scarlatti acts as the centre of Vomero, with the Piazza Vanvitelli at its heart.

More difficult to get to, Capodimonte is largely residential. Other than the Museo di Capodimonte, there should be no reason to warrant a visit. Exercise fanatics may want to check out the grounds around the museum – local joggers flock to the gardens for its clear air and lush greenery. Capodimonte is situated north of the Centro Storico.

Finally, for lovers of high fashion and even higher prices, Chiaia is the place to go. Located further west along the coast from the Port district, the streets around the Riviera di Chiaia – especially tiny Via Calabritto – hold exclusive Italian designer wear and interiors boutiques. The stroll along the Via Francesco Caracciolo towards Mergellina is especially loved by natives during the summer months due to the cooling Mediterranean breezes.

Those looking to get out of town should note that boats and hydrofoils bound for Procida, Ischia and Capri depart from the Molo Beverello in the Port district, while the Circumvesuviana trains towards Pompeii, Herculaneum and the Amalfi Coast leave from the Stazione Circumvesuviana and not the Stazione Centrale.

The city

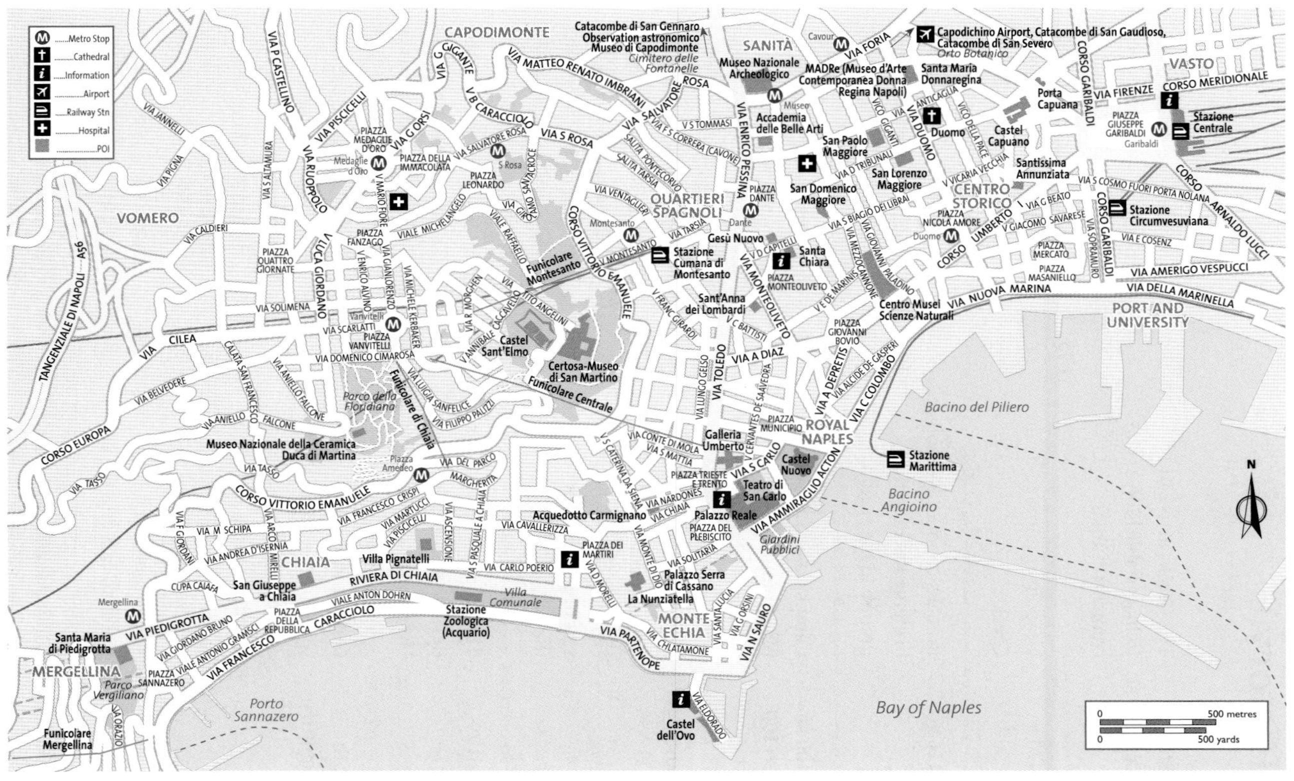

Metro Stop
Cathedral
Information
Airport
Railway Stn
Hospital
POI
0 500 metres
0 500 yards
N
Bay of Naples
Bacino del Piliero
Bacino Angioino
Porto Sannazero
PORT AND UNIVERSITY
ROYAL NAPLES
CENTRO STORICO
QUARTIERI SPAGNOLI
CAPODIMONTE
SANITÀ
VASTO
VOMERO
CHIAIA
MONTE ECHIA
MERGELLINA
Capodichino Airport, Catacombe di San Gaudioso, Catacombe di San Severo
Catacombe di San Gennaro
Observation astronomico
Museo di Capodimonte
Cimitero delle Fontanelle
Orto Botanico
Museo Nazionale Archeologico
Accademia delle Belle Arti
MADRe (Museo d'Arte Contemporanea Donna Regina Napoli)
Santa Maria Donnaregina
Duomo
Castel Capuano
Porta Capuana
Santissima Annunziata
San Paolo Maggiore
San Lorenzo Maggiore
San Domenico Maggiore
Gesù Nuovo
Santa Chiara
Centro Musei Scienze Naturali
Stazione Centrale
Stazione Circumvesuviana
Stazione Marittima
Stazione Cumana di Montesanto
Sant'Anna dei Lombardi
Castel Nuovo
Teatro di San Carlo
Galleria Umberto
Palazzo Reale
Giardini Pubblici
Palazzo Serra di Cassano
La Nunziatella
Castel dell'Ovo
Acquedotto Carmignano
Certosa-Museo di San Martino
Castel Sant'Elmo
Funicolare Montesanto
Funicolare Centrale
Funicolare di Chiaia
Parco della Floridiana
Museo Nazionale della Ceramica Duca di Martina
Villa Pignatelli
Villa Comunale
Stazione Zoologica (Acquario)
San Giuseppe a Chiaia
Santa Maria di Piedigrotta
Parco Vergiliano
Funicolare Mergellina
CORSO MERIDIONALE
CORSO GARIBALDI
VIA FIRENZE
PIAZZA GIUSEPPE GARIBALDI
Garibaldi
CORSO ARNALDO LUCCI
VIA S COSMO FUORI PORTA NOLANA
VIA AMERIGO VESPUCCI
VIA DELLA MARINELLA
VIA E COSENZ
VIA SOPRAMURO
VIA G BEATO
V GIACOMO SAVARESE
PIAZZA MERCATO
PIAZZA MASANIELLO
CORSO UMBERTO I
PIAZZA NICOLA AMORE
VIA NUOVA MARINA
VICO DELLA PACE
V VICARIA VECCHIA
ANTICAGLIA
VIA DUOMO
VICO GIGANTI
VIA D TRIBUNALI
VIA S BIAGIO DEI LIBRAI
VIA GIOVANNI PALADINO
VIA MEZZOCANNONE
V DE MARINIS
VIA FORIA
Cavour
Museo
Duomo
PIAZZA GIOVANNI BOVIO
VIA ALCIDE DE GASPERI
VIA C COLOMBO
VIA A DEPRETIS
VIA ENRICO PESSINA
PIAZZA DANTE
Dante
V D CAPITELLI
PIAZZA MONTEOLIVETO
VIA MONTEOLIVETO
V C BATTISTI
VIA A DIAZ
V CERVANTES DE SAAVEDRA
PIAZZA MUNICIPIO
VIA TOLEDO
VIA LUNGO GELSO
V FRANC GIRARDI
VIA S CARLO
VIA AMMIRAGLIO ACTON
PIAZZA TRIESTE E TRENTO
VIA CONTE DI MOLA
VIA S MATTIA
VIA NARDONES
VIA CHIAIA
PIAZZA DEL PLEBISCITO
VIA SOLITARIA
VIA G ORSINI
VIA SANTA LUCIA
VIA N SAURO
VIA ELDORADO
VIA CHIATAMONE
VIA MONTE DI DIO
V S CATERINA DA SIENA
VIA PARTENOPE
VIA D MORELLI
PIAZZA DEI MARTIRI
VIA CAVALLERIZZA
VIA CARLO POERIO
VIA S PASQUALE A CHIAIA
VIA ASCENSIONE
RIVIERA DI CHIAIA
VIALE ANTON DOHRN
VIA CARACCIOLO
PIAZZA DELLA REPUBBLICA
VIA FRANCESCO CRISPI
VIA MARTUCCI
VIA PISCICELLI
VIA ARCO MIRELLI
VIA ANDREA D'ISERNIA
VIA M SCHIPA
VIA F GIORDANI
CUPA CAIAFA
VIA PIEDIGROTTA
VIA GIORDANO BRUNO
VIALE ANTONIO GRAMSCI
VIA FRANCESCO
PIAZZA SANNAZERO
VIA ORAZIO
Mergellina
VIA TASSO
CORSO EUROPA
TANGENZIALE DI NAPOLI
A56
VIA BELVEDERE
VIA ANIELLO FALCONE
CALATA SAN FRANCESCO
CORSO VITTORIO EMANUELE
Piazza Amedeo
VIA DEL PARCO MARGHERITA
VIA FILIPPO PALIZZI
VIA LUIGIA SANFELICE
VIA MICHELE KERBAKER
VIA GIANLORENZO
PIAZZA VANVITELLI
Vanvitelli
VIA SCARLATTI
V ENRICO ALVINO
VIA DOMENICO CIMAROSA
VIA CILEA
VIA SOLIMENA
V LUCA GIORDANO
PIAZZA QUATTRO GIORNATE
PIAZZA FANZAGO
V MARIO FIORE
PIAZZA MEDAGLIE D'ORO
Medaglie d'Oro
VIA RUOPPOLO
VIA PISCICELLI
VIA P CASTELLINO
VIA S ALTAMURA
VIA CALDIERI
VIA JANNELLI
VIA PIGNA
VIA G ORSI
PIAZZA DELLA IMMACOLATA
VIA SALVATORE ROSA
S Rosa
PIAZZA LEONARDO
VIALE MICHELANGELO
VIA G GIGANTE
V B CARACCIOLO
VIA S ROSA
RAMO SANTACROCE
VIA GIRO
VIALE RAFFAELLO
VIA TITO ANGELINI
VIA CACCAVELLO
V ANNIBALE
VIA R MORGHEN
VIA MATTEO RENATO IMBRIANI
SALITA PONTECORVO
SALITA TARSIA
VIA VENTAGLIERI
Montesanto
VIA MONTESANTO
VIA TARSIA
VIA S CORREA (CAVONE)
V S TOMMASI
VIA SALVATORE ROSA

History

8th century BC	The Greeks arrive in Ischia, establishing a colony at Cuma.
470 BC	Neapolis is founded by the Greeks.
326 BC	Romans conquer Neapolis, bringing the Roman Empire to the region.
100 BC**–** AD **100**	Campania becomes the playground of the rich of the Roman Empire.
AD **27–37**	Emperor Tiberius arrives in Capri and decides to stay. The Roman Empire's seat of power is moved to the island.
AD **79**	The eruption of Vesuvius destroys Pompeii and Herculaneum.
5th century	Goths and Vandals take sporadic control of the city, leaving desecration and destruction in their wake.
536	The Byzantine Emperor Justinian captures the city.
581, 592 and 599	Lombards and Saracens lay siege to Naples – the invaders are defeated each time.
645	Basilio becomes the first native Duke of Neapolis, and the city flourishes under his rule.
1062–77	The Normans take Capua, Amalfi and Salerno.
1130	Roger II – a Norman – is crowned King of Sicily.
1139	Neapolitans swear allegiance to the Sicilian crown. Naples falls into decline as power and revenue travel to Palermo. The city's population is 30,000.
1194	The end of the Norman line. Tancred, last Norman ruler of Naples, dies. Henry of Swabia, the son of the Holy Roman Emperor, takes control. He becomes King Henry I of Sicily.
1214	Frederick II becomes King of Southern Italy and Holy Roman Emperor upon the death of his father Henry I. Under his leadership, a

university is founded in 1224.

1251 The death of Frederick II divides the city as Naples declares itself a free commune. After a long siege, the Imperial forces of German King Conrad (son of Frederick) win back the city in 1253.

1256 Sicily is taken by Charles of Anjou, beginning a brief period of French reign. The capital is moved from Palermo back to Naples.

1302 Sicily is given by Charles of Anjou to the Aragonese.

1442 Alfonso of Aragon takes control of Sicily. Southern Italy is unified once again.

1494 France's King Charles VIII occupies the city on the invitation of the noble classes. The Neapolitan people rebel and reinstate the Aragonese King, Ferdinand II.

1502 The first of the hated Spanish viceroys rules the city as Ferdinand III leaves. Viceroys continue to rule over Naples for the next 250 years.

1600 Naples, with its population of 300,000, becomes Europe's largest city.

1606 Caravaggio, fleeing Rome, arrives in Naples. His influence on local art is enormous.

1631 Vesuvius erupts and 3,500 are killed.

1647 Local stallholder and fisherman Masaniello declares revolution in the city, protesting against crippling Spanish taxes. Nine days later he is assassinated, yet revolts continue across the region.

1656 Plague kills three-quarters of the population, and the local economy is devastated. The Baroque period begins, as survivors attempt to replace the everyday with the ornate.

1707 Naples is occupied by Austria. Viceroys continue to rule for the next 27 years.

1734 Charles Bourbon, son of Philip V of Spain, expels the Austrians and becomes Charles III of Sicily. Naples is reinstated as the capital.

1737	Teatro di San Carlo, Italy's oldest theatre, is built.
1748	The excavations of Pompeii and Herculaneum commence.
1757	King Charles abdicates to succeed his father as King of Spain.
1768	Ferdinand, son of Charles, marries Maria Carolina – the daughter of the Austrian Empress. By 1777, she ousts all reformers and backs the leadership of Briton Sir John Acton. Acton eventually takes over running the kingdom in all but name.
1798	Rome is taken from the French by the Neapolitans – for exactly 11 days.
1799	The royal family flees on Nelson's ship to Sicily after invasion by the French. Intellectuals back a republic, while working classes remain staunchly royalist. Ferdinand returns following defeat of the republicans. Two hundred rebels are executed.
1806	France takes Naples again – this time under the leadership of Joseph Bonaparte. Royals escape to Sicily.
1816	Royals return to Naples and Ferdinand resumes his rule.
1820	Uprising by the Carbonari group forces Ferdinand to grant a constitution.
1821	Austrian troops invade on the invitation of Ferdinand in order to quash constitutional government.
1848	Naples' Parliament demands a constitution. A year later, Ferdinand's son dissolves government.
1860	Naples joins the United Kingdom of Italy after Garibaldi and the unification troops enter the city.
1880–1914	Two and a half million Italians – mostly from the south – emigrate to North America.
1884	Serious cholera outbreak forces the city to examine infrastructure and housing issues.
1943	Allied bombs destroy Naples. Citizens liberate

	the city in the Quattro Giornate Napoletane. Germans ruin infrastructure as they flee the city.
1943–9	One-third of Neapolitan women are forced into prostitution. The *camorra* (mafia) and black market begin their reign of terror.
1944	Vesuvius erupts, killing 26.
1946	National referendum ousts the Italian monarchy against the wishes of the Neapolitan public.
1950–93	The Christian Democrat party rules the city. Many candidates are backed by the powerful *camorra* clans. Unregulated development and industrialisation transform the city.
1971	A government report finds that most post-war buildings are both illegal and unsafe.
1973	Cholera hits the city again.
1980	Three thousand people are killed and thousands more are left homeless when an earthquake rocks the city.
1992	*Mani Pulite* (clean hands) anti-corruption campaign is launched.
1993	Left-winger Antonio Bassolino is elected mayor.
1994	The G7 summit is held in the city.
2001	The Global Forum is held in Naples. Anti-globalisation riots rock the city. Over 100 are injured.
2006	Scientists from the US National Academy of Sciences warn that the next eruption of Vesuvius could cause massive devastation. Italy win the football World Cup for the fourth time.
2007	*Gomorrah*, Roberto Saviano's scathing exposé of the *camorra*, leads to death threats and an acclaimed film.
2008	Rubbish crisis leads to clashes between police and local protesters. Troops sent in to help police fight the *camorra*.
2009	Over 100,000 people march through Naples in one of the biggest anti-mafia protests of recent years.

Politics

The Italian Republic was formed in 1946 following the banishment of Vittorio Emanuele (son of Italy's last king, Umberto II). Over 50 governments have been elected since the first Italian government was formed under the leadership of Naples-born Enrico de Nicola.

The government

The country is governed by a parliamentary system (*Parlamento*), based in the Italian capital of Rome, and consisting of a Senate (*Senato della Republica*) and the Chamber of Deputies (*Camera dei Deputati*). The executive branch is made up of an elected chief of state – currently President Giorgio Napolitano, who was born in Naples in 1926. The President appoints a Prime Minister and confirms the appointment with the Parliament. Right-wing Forza Italia leader and Italy's foremost entrepreneur Silvio Berlusconi currently holds the post.

The head of state is the President, who is elected by an electoral college consisting of both Houses of Parliament and 58 regional representatives. The Prime Minister acts as the head of government, referred to in Italy as President of the Council of Ministers. The Council of Ministers acts as the Italian cabinet, with posts being appointed by the Prime Minister and approved by the President. A coalition government alliance consisting of the Popolo della Libertà and the Separatist Lega Nord currently controls power.

There are 315 seats in the Houses of Senate, of which 232 are directly elected and 83 elected by regional proportional representation. Seats are held for a term of five years. A limited number of members-for-life, including former Presidents of the Republic, also hold seats. The 630 members of the lower house serve five-year terms, of which 475 are directly elected, with 155 by proportional representation.

The republic is divided into 20 regions or counties. Naples is the administrative capital of the county of Campania. The surrounding areas of Amalfi, Ischia, Capri, and the ruins of Pompeii and Herculaneum, are also within Campania's borders.

Local government

For 50 years following the end of World War II, Naples was controlled by the

Christian Democrats, who were backed by the economic and political might of the crime-fuelled *camorra* clans. Most of Naples' crumbling post-war architecture can be attributed to the unregulated and illegal construction undertaken by mafia-controlled developers. Local leaders and police forces turned a blind eye, until the earthquake of 1980 destroyed acres of property due to the poor building codes and practices maintained by shady construction companies.

A city of rebellion

Between 1983 and 1993, ten mayors succeeded each other during the post-quake chaos. During this problematic decade, public services ground to a halt. Only 300 buses served a population of over 2 million, and rubbish collection was left to constantly striking *camorra*-backed conglomerates.

The national 'clean hands' campaign – launched in 1993 – provided the impetus needed to bring about the dawn of a new Neapolitan Renaissance. Communist Antonio Bassolino was voted in as mayor, narrowly defeating the campaign of Alessandra Mussolini, granddaughter of the wartime leader. Under Bassolino's control, the city enjoyed a massive clean-up, restoring the Centro Storico in time for the 1994 G7 summit meeting. After gaining re-election in 1997, Bassolino lost much of his popular support as cracks among his fractured coalition of aligned parties began to show. Naples' first female mayor, Rosa Russo Jervolino, stepped into City Hall in 2001. Unfortunately, she too is hampered by a coalition government who spend more time arguing among themselves than they do in passing public policies and developing projects.

A city built on disasters

Many cities have experienced periods of tragedy – yet few have come back from the number of disasters and volume of destruction thrust upon the poor citizens of Naples. Lava, disease and earthquakes have all attempted to flatten the city at some point during its history, yet locals keep coming back for more.

Thar' she blows

Until the deadly blast of AD 79, travellers, merchants and farmers visiting the Campanian coastline were drawn to the area because of its unusually fertile soil. While farmers realised that the nutrient-rich earth owed its value to the volcanic activity of Vesuvius, few could have seen that the price tag attached to this rural splendour would cost so much in lives. Even after the devastation of 79, little was done to prevent future calamities – the natural beauty, fabulous farmland and convenient ports made sure residents would choose to stick it out rather than give up their precious homelands.

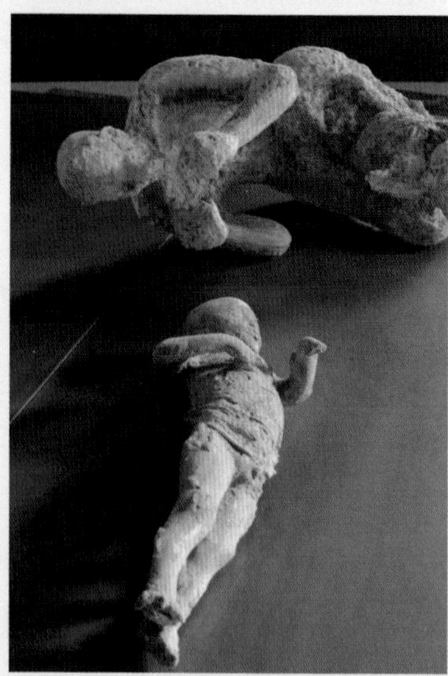

Victims of the disaster at Pompeii

But volcanoes and red-hot lava aren't the only things that have threatened Naples during its 2,400-year history. At various times, Naples has been decimated by plague, cholera, earthquakes, bombings, war and famine. Modern-day Neapolitans have yet to learn the lessons of the past, as a number of local deaths can be attributed to shoddy post-war construction practices that resulted in the collapse of thousands of buildings and continued crumbling masonry following the 'quake of 1980.

Unlike future-thinking, earthquake-prone nations like Japan, Italy – specifically the city of Naples – does little to ensure that buildings don't collapse during an earth tremor. While the laws are in place, the mafia

Mount Vesuvius

constantly flouts them. Until 1993, local newspaper headlines reported on construction scandals on an almost daily basis. Winning a seat in the Campanian government was like writing yourself a blank cheque, as long as you worked together with the *camorra* clans and didn't get caught by a periodic police raid or investigative journalist.

Chaos reigns

The threat of daily destruction is reflected in the way Neapolitans choose to live their lives. Traffic chaos rules supreme, business appointments are often minutes, if not hours, later than they are scheduled for, a lunch could take you well into the late hours of the evening and building developments go up higgledy-piggledy on every corner of land possible. Of course, this lifestyle choice often results in even more destruction and calamity, but you might as well be surrounded by splendid Baroque architecture, rather than a soulless, yet earthquake-proof, high-rise.

CENTRO DIREZIONALE

As the rest of the world profited from the 'greed is good' era of the 1980s, Naples fell into a state of serious decline. Desperate to attract big business, the local government launched the city's largest ever publicly managed construction project – the Centro Direzionale. Designed by Japanese architect Kenzo Tange, the Centro Direzionale comprises a series of ultra-modern skyscrapers with an emphasis on the glass and concrete popular during the flashy 1980s. Situated on a stretch of isolated, marshy land cleared by the bombs of World War II, the project never really took off as the anticipated injection of capital failed to materialise. Delays, bribery and scandal continue to plague the project, remaining far from completion to this day.

Culture and festivals

The citizens of Naples are of the 'work-to-live' mindset, revelling in the parties, festivals and religious occasions that bring a halt to major sections of the city on a daily basis. You won't need to give a Neapolitan too many excuses to knock off early for the day – especially when faced with the typically glorious weather and crystal-clear panoramas that characterise the surrounding countryside.

Religion

If you think that there's a church on every corner in Naples, then you'd probably be right. While many churches are still used as houses of worship, over 50 per cent of Neapolitan religious centres are boarded up – whether due to floods, bombings, disrepair or earthquakes.

When visiting a church, it is best to be soberly attired – remember that these sites are active places of religious practice. Try not to visit during Mass unless you feel you can blend in with the congregation. Masses are always conducted in Italian or – more rarely – Latin, so if you don't speak the lingo then you may be at a loss trying to follow the service.

Neapolitans would like to think that religion continues to play an important part of everyday life, and in many ways it does – for the older generations, at least. As a staunchly Roman Catholic city, many local customs and laws acknowledge church doctrine, yet embrace the modern requirements of western society.

Due to the disasters that continually befall the city, Neapolitan Christianity has evolved into a mishmash of ancient superstition, belief in miraculous occurrences and cultish behaviour. Many believers continue to pray to the skulls of the deceased, and the bulk of the population still adheres to the prophecies that revolve around the annual liquefaction of the blood of San Gennaro. If San Gennaro's blood doesn't start flowing, then it might as well be raining toads from the heavens. Everything from a Napoli football team loss to nuclear war will be blamed on the fact that the annual miracle failed to transpire.

Body language

Neapolitans are famous for their body language. In a culture as macho as this one, most of the arm-flailing, finger pointing and shouting you spot will probably be more for show than anything else. Most arguments you see will be a result of traffic accidents – more common than you might think. So if you find that you experience a fender-bender, the best course of action is to apologise profusely while the other driver lets off a bit of steam, even if the crash isn't your fault.

Though on the increase, English is not commonly spoken by locals. You will find that tourist traps, popular restaurants, shops and hotels will understand the basics, but when it comes down to the nitty-gritty of directions and information, you'll often be left to your own devices.

Nightlife

If you're planning a night out on the town, you might want to catch some sleep during the evening. Most nights don't get going until the wee hours of the morning. Nightclubs and cafés may be open throughout the evening, but you'll find them empty and lacking in atmosphere until at least midnight. Early dinners are unheard of in this town. In many cases you will find restaurants locked tight during the hours when you traditionally enjoy your last meal of the day.

One of the nicest things to do is to take a simple stroll along the seaside or through the Centro Storico at night. While the streets aren't well lit, you'll find plenty of couples enjoying the night air.

Major festivals

The two major festivals celebrated in Naples are Christmas and the feast of the city's patron saint, San Gennaro, held on 19 September.

Christmas is a beautiful time to visit the city. Shopping reaches an almost frenzied pace in the streets

Naples' Duomo

around San Gregorio Armeno where locals stock up on figures for their traditional Nativity scenes. Almost every church in town has a Christmas crib, the finest being in the Palazzo Reale and in San Martino.

The feast of San Gennaro, while less important religiously to the world at large, seemingly controls and foretells the fortunes of the two million people who call Naples home. According to tradition, the blood of San Gennaro is supposed to liquefy on 19 September every year to honour his day as patron saint of the city. Frantic praying continues throughout the day at the Duomo, as black-clad devotees cluster around the gory artefact. Tradition says that if the blood fails to liquefy, then the upcoming year is sure to be a bad one.

Footie fanatics

While not strictly a holiday, you will find that the city screeches to a halt whenever the local football team, SSC Napoli, has a match. While far from the glory days of the late 1980s when Argentinian superstar Maradona led the team to its first ever *scudetto* (league title), the Stadio San Paolo still manages to pull in fans. Poor

SSC Napoli fans head off to Stadio San Paolo

MATCH-DAY MADNESS

Footie has been taking over the hearts and minds of Neapolitans since 1905 when the crew of an English cargo ship challenged a team of local dignitaries to a match. The British connection remained throughout Naples' early love affair with the sport right up until 1926 when local team SSC Napoli was founded under the direction of their first manager, Englishman Willy Garbutt.

If you're a fan of footie, then there's no better place to watch a match than from the grandstands of Stadio San Paolo. While tickets on match day are like gold dust, there are always plenty of touts hanging around outside the stadium to part you from your hard-earned cash.

management decisions relegated once-mighty Napoli to the Third Division; however, fortunes have risen of late with the team finally promoted to the elite Serie A at the end of the 2006/07 season. National football hero Fabio Cannavaro is a local boy and used to play for Napoli. The supporters are known as Mastiffs and follow their team religiously.

Quiet conservatism

Italian morals are decidedly anachronistic, especially in the south. While the north votes conservative and thinks liberally, Naples and the surrounding countryside vote communist and think conservatively. Much of this attitude is due to the strong influence that the Roman Catholic Church wields in the area. Neapolitans are generally tolerant towards racial, religious and sexual minorities, choosing to ignore any obvious displays of 'individuality' rather than express any formal disdain.

Hearth and home

Chivalry remains alive and well in Naples. This is a town where young men still get up out of their seats on public transport for the benefit of a woman of any age. At the heart of Neapolitan life is the family. Respect for elders remains strong, so if you exhibit the slightest sign of a wrinkle, you'll find Neapolitan youth extremely accommodating.

Children are especially loved by one and all. Prepare your son or daughter – if you are bringing them along – for much cheek-pinching, cooing and general admiration. Complete strangers love to dote over a baby, with some holding packages of sweets just for the purpose of giving them to your cherubic child.

Architecture

The history of Naples stretches as far back as the days of the Greek Empire, and so does its architecture. Once Europe's most populous city, residents have slept in grottoes, alleyways, warehouses and churchyards at any given period, depending upon their place in society. Its rapidly growing population meant architects needed to design residences that built up rather than out. Look up when you walk through the streets to see the results.

THE PALAZZI OF VIA TOLEDO

A walk down the Via Toledo today will confront you with a plethora of high-street shops, department stores, cafés and *tabacchi* alcoves. Yet it wasn't always like this. Via Toledo used to be the address of choice for the rich and powerful of the city.

The popularity of Via Toledo as a place to live occurred following the extension of the city walls during the Renaissance. Today, most of the grand structures are crumbling and far from their prime, but you can still glimpse signs of former grandeur in the form of Palazzo Buono, the **Palazzo Berio** (No 256) and the **Palazzo Barbaja** (No 205), which was once home to composer Gioacchino Rossini of *The Barber of Seville* opera fame.

The Greek influence

Remnants of Greek architecture are difficult to find within greater Naples. For glimpses of ancient Athenian rule, you'll have to go into the Campanian countryside to the temples of Paestum and Cuma. Little remains from the days when a prosperous settlement known as Paleopolis covered the area, but its influences remain.

The Roman age

Romans followed many of the original Greek plans, especially their main roads and intersections. Piazza Bellini, while a hub of activity and life today, originally marked the edge of Greek city limits – the original city walls can be found 1m (3ft) under the ground at this point.

Two of the most important churches in the city lie directly above important hubs of Roman life. Located under the Duomo and the church of San Lorenzo Maggiore are artefacts from Roman market life, while the original Roman

Monastic cemetery, Certosa di San Martino

The quiet conservatism of Naples today is very different from ruined Pompeii's famed licentiousness

baths have been included in a museum built behind the church of Santa Chiara.

For the best examples of Roman architecture, you should make the trip to Pompeii and Herculaneum. These preserved towns, destroyed during the eruption of Vesuvius in AD 79, should tell you everything you will probably ever want to know about the period – and more.

From the Normans to the Baroque

After the Normans named Naples as the capital of Sicily in the 11th century, a flurry of building activity was set in motion. Castel dell'Ovo and Castel Capuano were built to provide homes and fortifications for the leaders of the kingdom, while city walls were pushed out to increase the size of the blossoming metropolis. Church construction also experienced a boom during this period, with local masons enjoying a period of high employment unheard of during any age since that time. Gothic architecture was the style of choice, with examples evident in the designs of the Duomo, Santa Maria Donnaregina, San Lorenzo and Sant'Eligio.

The Renaissance left its mark on the city in many ways during the period of the Aragon court: the finest documentation of the movement is in the *Tavola Strozzi*, located in the Certosa di San Martino museum.

A lotto luck

Although the Catholic Church would like you to think otherwise, superstition and luck have a powerful hold over the mind of the average Neapolitan. On many street corners you will find tarot readers plying their trade, and many residents pay a visit to their favourite fortune tellers as often as they go out to get a loaf of bread.

Misfortune and destruction – specifically in the form of earthquakes and volcanoes – while scientifically proven to be caused by the geological faults and volcanic activity in the area, are often blamed on the supernatural. Keeping your *monacello* (house spirit) happy is one way to ensure your continued good fortune. Taking the form of a mischievous little boy, the *monacello* tells your fortune depending on what he chooses to wear. If he is dressed in white, then you have a bountiful future. Red, however, means impending doom.

A good-luck symbol in ceramic tile

The 'evil eye' is still thought of as an everyday problem. One common method by which those afflicted with bad mojo remove the problem is through a local TV show on which local *maghi* (magicians) appear so that people can ring in and ask for their evil spirits to be removed. If a *mago* isn't available and a Neapolitan feels like they've had an encounter with a *jettatore* (spell caster), then their best course of action is to touch iron, or a horn of gold, coral or silver. 'Making horns' by pointing the index and little finger at a suspected caster is another sure-fire preventative measure, although it is also highly offensive if performed on an innocent bystander.

Small pieces of horn or iron in the shape of a smiling *jettatore* are available from most souvenir stores if you feel the need for a bit of luck. Taxi drivers are particularly well stocked with charms, mainly due to the poor driving habits of the city's inhabitants.

Historically, extreme poverty and natural disasters have provided Neapolitans with good reasons to believe in anything they can in order to survive. This explains why the lottery proved to be extremely popular when it was first introduced. After all, what other organisation combined the superstitious power of numbers with the opportunity to get rich? Neapolitans play the lottery with a fervour seen only in the most dedicated of religious followers. There are 90 numbers to choose from, with many locals refusing to leave the country whenever a big draw is approaching or tell even their closest relations their favourite series of digits. As expected in superstitious Naples, all of the numbers in *Il Lotto* hold a specific meaning in order to assist with their selection. A handbook known as the *smorfia*, which outlines the separate meanings, details the language of the numbers in relation to nightly dreams. If you need help picking the right combination, go along to any lotto office and relay the details of your dreams to the ticket seller, who will then analyse the dreams and find the right numbers that match the images. Some of the more intriguing numbers include 85 (Souls of Purgatory), 45 (wine), 76 (fountain) and 2 (little girl). There are even selections available should your dreams prove to be X-rated, including 28 (breasts), 29 (penis) and 16 (bottom).

The golden horns symbol is thought to bring good luck

Piazza Dante and eponymous statue

Baroque bonanza

Never before or since has an architectural or design aesthetic captured the Neapolitan attitude as much as the Baroque period. The fantastical and ostentatious elements of Baroque combined perfectly with the Neapolitan flair for the dramatic. As such, the city is awash with examples of Baroque fancy. From the stunning Reggia at Caserta, built by Vanvitelli for the royal family of Naples, to the grotesque skulls littering the front of the church of Santa Maria del Purgatorio, Naples can sometimes resemble a celebration of the extreme – all characteristic of this decidedly ostentatious and sometimes gaudy period in architectural history.

Piazza Dante, the San Carlo opera house, Albergo dei Poveri (Europe's largest ever civic construction) and the imposing Palazzo Reale all date their births to the years of the Bourbon dynasty when passions and coffers overflowed.

Architectural big names to look out for include Vaccaro, the aforementioned Vanvitelli, Fuga, Sanfelice and Medrano. Most of the major Baroque projects of the time can be attributed to one of these big names in building design.

HUNTING FOR GLAMOUR

Naples owes much of its stunning Baroque architecture to the Bourbon family's love of a good hunt. Determined to bag as many trophies as they possibly could, architects were hired by the noble classes to build the Reggia at Caserta and the stunning villas along the Miglio d'Oro in order to provide easy access to the countryside. Today, the Reggia rivals Versailles in terms of both size and scope. The Italian armed forces now claim many of the rooms in the palace for administrative purposes, so you could say that guns remain an important fixture in this regal residence of times past.

Onwards from Napoleon

Following Napoleon's successful capture of the city in the early 19th century, Naples went into an architectural decline that has remained until the present day. French forces, in an effort to control the disease and crowded conditions of the city, focused most of their energies on urban renewal, wiping out hundreds of dilapidated neighbourhoods in order to replace them with open areas, squares and gardens in a neoclassical style. The seafront found a new lease of life, with the Chiaia district announcing its status as a favourable address – an honour it has yet to give up. And engineering feats like the invention of the funicular opened up high-ground locations like Vomero to residential development.

Following the destructive bombs of World War II, developers either rebuilt ancient structures according to original plans or replaced entire neighbourhoods with horrific modern eyesores denounced by locals. Residents had little say in what was going up around them during this boom period, as most of the construction blueprints were in the hands of the mafia and the pockets of local government. Huge council-housing estates in the suburbs of the city transformed the outskirts into crime-filled wastelands of poverty, while factories gutted the seashore – convenient for the dumping of pollution and waste, but not so attractive for the average tourist to look at.

Notable buildings from this period include the horrific Jolly Hotel complex, the abandoned steelworks at Bagnoli and the massive Centro Direzionale project of the 1980s. Plans are afoot to transform Bagnoli into a museum, leisure park and marina complex, but the project is years away from completion.

Albergo dei Poveri

Impressions

Naples is quite a broad city, squished lengthways along the Bay of Naples by the hills of Capodimonte, Vomero and Vesuvius. Walking around these neighbourhoods is extremely easy, but distances between varying districts can be a bit of a trek. The city is neither pedestrian- nor traffic-friendly. A new, extensive metro system is doing a little to alleviate the legendary traffic jams that cripple the city centre, but there are still vast areas that aren't served by the new lines.

City layout

Other than the winding streets of the Centro Storico and the distinctive hills of Capodimonte and Vomero, Neapolitan neighbourhoods aren't all that well defined. Residents of Chiaia, with their seaside views and boutiques, tend to be slightly snobbier than those who dwell in the industrial wastelands of the Port and University. Meanwhile, the communities of Toledo and Sanità are overwhelmingly close-knit.

Plans to modernise the beleaguered Port and University district have been under way for years. If the project ever gets off the ground, then entire tracts of disused factories and industrial wasteland will be cleared to allow locals the possibility of reclaiming the Bay of Naples.

When to go

Peak season in Naples is during the summer. Crowds pack the city streets and temperatures soar. Savvy locals get out of town fast during the months of July and August, doing as the tourists do by flocking to the Amalfi Coast and the islands of Capri and Ischia.

Spring and autumn are invariably pleasant. Temperatures rarely drop much below 20°C (68°F) and occasional rainstorms leave the city and the views from Vomero crystal clear. The offshore islands are best in March and October: there may be fewer hotels and restaurant options, but the crowds will be gone and there is often a good chance of experiencing freak summer-like weather.

From November to February, temperatures drop, sometimes to almost 0°C (32°F). A light dusting of snow can often be spotted on the top of Vesuvius and the air is clear and sweet. Occasional periods of grey, dreary weather hit the city during this period, only to leave a few days later.

Getting around

Until all the lines on the new metro system are completed (phase 2 is due to be finished in 2011), visitors will have to rely on taxis, buses and their two feet. While the city is relatively compact, it does stretch a fair way along the Bay of Naples, making a full day of walking an exhausting prospect.

Taxis can be found at ranks dotted throughout the city. While inexpensive compared to the fares of other major cities, drivers are notorious for their scams. Be sure to insist that the meter is turned on before you depart.

Buses are plentiful in Naples, with almost all the lines running from the bus depot outside Piazza Garibaldi.

Mornings on the Med – Naples Port

Give yourself lots of time if using this option, however, as the buses stop at almost every corner in the city.

For longer distances, trains and ferries are the way to go. With Capri, Procida and Ischia you have no other option than to use the boats that leave the mainland on an almost hourly basis. Long-distance train services to Rome and the other major centres of Italy arrive and depart from Stazione Centrale in Piazza Garibaldi. Journeys along the Campania coastline to Pompeii, Herculaneum, Amalfi and Sorrento depart from the Stazione Circumvesuviana on Corso Garibaldi. Trains run regularly throughout the day until about midnight.

Driving in the city

Driving in Naples is legendarily awful. Tiny streets, crumbling asphalt, constant repaving and a high reliance on automobiles and scooters as a form of transport combine to bring the city's transport to a crawl.

In the summer, the streets of Ischia, Procida, Sorrento and the Amalfi Coast are absolutely jammed, especially at weekends. If you must bring your car, make sure to do so on weekdays only. On many Sundays vehicular traffic is banned. Check with your concierge or car rental agency to confirm dates.

Pollution and litter

If you're used to clean streets and tree-lined avenues, then you may be in for a shock. The streets of Naples can sometimes resemble a refuse dump. The paralysing traffic does little to help the situation, with air pollution rising to levels that asthmatics may find difficult to deal with. When everything becomes a bit too untidy for comfort, flee to the more subdued neighbourhoods of Vomero or Capodimonte. The hillside perches of these two districts provide a release from the smog.

Manners and mores

Neapolitans are a blunt, relaxed and passionate people. If you meet a local in the street, don't be surprised if they give you a hug or peck on the cheek. Personal space areas are much smaller in Naples than you may be used to at home. If excited, Neapolitans will gesticulate, using body language to emphasise their point.

If you are going out on the town, plan for a long evening. Waiters are happy for you to take your time over your meal and will do as little as possible to present you with something as annoying as a bill. Meals are intended to be savoured. If in a rush, you will have to emphasise this fact to the staff as often as possible.

The cost of living

Italy has a reputation for being an expensive place to visit. Naples and the rest of the south are relatively affordable, as they are situated in the less wealthy half of the country. The exception to this rule occurs in the heavily touristed areas of Capri, Ischia and the Amalfi Coast.

Naples transport system

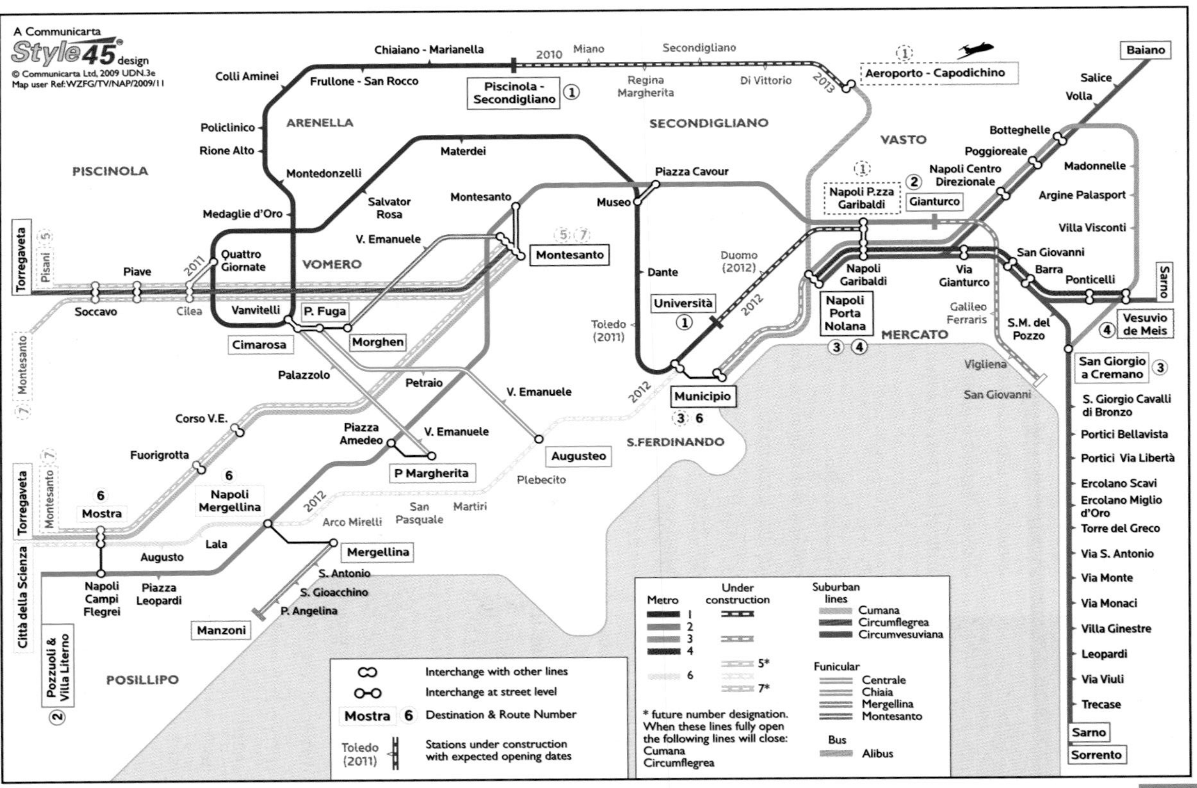

Naples: Royal Naples and Chiaia

If you like centres of royal domination, ancient history, rambling fishermen's quarters and lands stained by the blood of conquering forces, then Royal Naples is the district to explore. The site of Neapolitan power and government since the day the city was founded over 2,400 years ago, Royal Naples is home to more regal tourist treasures than any other part of town.

Filled with piazze and palazzi, this traffic-free district is packed with royal relics and elegant shopping. Important buildings range in size from the huge to the absolutely enormous, in keeping with the egos of the residents who originally called this corner of the city home – the Neapolitan royal families.

Legends and lore

Legend has it that a group of sailors discovered the body of the siren Parthenope washed up on the rocks at this point on the Campanian coastline. Distraught after having her affections turned down by Ulysses, the mermaid drowned herself, only to have her corpse drift back to shore. In an act of charity, the sailors decided to bury her body on the rock, and thus gave the name of Parthenope (or Paleopolis) to the original settlement.

The development of the city of Naples occurred after the Greeks, who settled on the islands of Megaris and Monte Echia – where Castel dell'Ovo still sits – decided to move inland to form a new town or 'Neapolis'.

Acquedotto Carmignano

Naples' most intriguing tour takes you underground and through the various tunnels, cisterns and wells that make up the city's water system. The Carmignano drainage system was designed and built during the 16th- and 17th-century reign of the Spanish viceroys. Naples' population was expanding at a massive rate, and a method was needed to bring constant supplies of fresh water to newly expanded districts.

Hour-long tours take you to 40m (130ft) below the city centre, past alcoves used as air-raid shelters in World War II. Trainers or comfortable shoes are strongly recommended. This is definitely not an experience for the claustrophobic!

Via Chiaia 1–2 (Bar Gambrinus). Tel: 081 400 256; www.lanapolisotterranea.it. Tours: Thur

9pm, Sat 10am, noon, 6pm, Sun 10am, 11am, noon, 6pm. Admission charge. Bus: 24, C22, C82, R2.

Castel dell'Ovo

Naples' oldest castle, this imposing seafront structure boasts over a thousand years of history. Built during the Norman period, Castel dell'Ovo was originally intended for military use, defending the city from the almost constant threat of invasion and terror. Its site was always an important location in Neapolitan history – it originally held a monastic community during the Middle Ages. Before that, it was a treasured section of the grounds owned by the Roman General Lucullus. Legend says that Castel dell'Ovo derived its name from the Roman period when the poet Virgil stayed as a guest of Lucullus. According to tradition, Virgil buried a magical egg in the foundations, predicting doom for Naples should the egg ever break.

Many of the rooms in the Castel dell'Ovo are in use as offices; however, there are still large sections of the structure undergoing restoration. Even when there are crowds of tourists, the castle can feel strangely deserted. To get the most out of it, lose yourself in the maze of quiet passageways and landings, making sure you climb up the long ramp inside the castle to enjoy the views of the Bay below.

Via Partenope. Tel: 081 240 0055. Open: Mon–Sat 8am–7.30pm, Sun 8am–2pm. Bus: 140, C24, C25, C28, R3. Tram: 1.

Castel Nuovo

Built in 1279 by Charles of Anjou, the Castel Nuovo (New Castle) was the Angevin residence and fortress of choice. Little of the original decoration exists inside the castle walls, thanks to a series of alterations performed during the age of the Aragonese (15th century).

During its Angevin heyday, the Castel Nuovo was a centre for the arts, with beacons of the worlds of literature and visual art drawn to the Neapolitan court. Boccaccio's epic collection of Italian lore, the *Decameron*, was written during this period, as well as a number of short stories set in and around the city of Naples. In addition, Giotto famously frescoed the castle's chapel and main entrance hall. Unfortunately, little of Giotto's work remains on display, with the exception of the work found on the ceiling of the Sala dei Baroni (Room of the Barons) – scene of Naples' rambunctious city council meetings. While the council meetings have a tendency to get vicious, they will never be as deadly as the events in 1486 when a group of mutinous barons was murdered by King Ferrante, thus giving the room its name.

For authentic Angevin architecture, your best option is the **Cappella Palatina** – it is the only section of this castle that was left untouched by the meddling Aragonese.

Preparations are slowly proceeding to continue with restorations of the castle, including plans to open up the dungeons, construct a lift in the northeastern tower and excavate the **Fossa del Coccodrillo** (Drain of the Crocodile) – a room in which a large crocodile apparently devoured particularly dangerous enemies of the state.

Piazza Municipio. Tel: 081 795 5877. Open: Mon–Sat 9am–7pm, Sun 9am–2.30pm; ticket office closes 1hr earlier. Admission charge. Bus: C25, E3, R1, R2, R3. Tram: 1.

Galleria Umberto

A vaulted glass- and steel-covered shopping arcade similar in style and design to the Galleria in Milan, this indoor wallet-busting mall is packed with a number of upmarket boutiques catering to the tourist trade. Today, renovations are under way to replace a number of missing glass panes.

The Galleria Umberto

From Piazza Trieste e Trento to Via Toledo. Bus: 24, C22, C82, R2, R3.

Monte Echia

The home of ancient Paleopolis sits above the crater rim of an extinct volcano. Located southwest of Piazza del Plebiscito, Monte Echia is the oldest section of the city, dating back to the days when this tiny dot-on-the-map was an unimportant settlement on the edge of the Greek Empire. The end of the Greek age and the success of the Roman Empire proved to be a boon for Paleopolis – by this time renamed Neapolis – as famous citizens from the capital were drawn to the area's natural beauty and healing waters. In the 1st century BC, the great Roman General Lucullus owned much of Monte Echia, building an extensive villa complex that stretched from the shoreline across as far as Mergellina.

Military might

Monte Echia's military connections remain strong – both the police headquarters and a military academy look out over this cradle of western civilisation. Views of the bay can still be enjoyed from the terrace of a decidedly run-down garden at the top of the hill just off Salita Echia.

La Nunziatella

Visit this tiny Baroque church to understand the saying 'size isn't everything'. Built for the Bourbon royal family in 1787, La Nunziatella

features a beautiful marble altar and uniquely tiled flooring. Today, the church is owned and used by the military academy located next door.
Via Generale Parisi 16. Tel: 081 764 1520. Open: Sun 9–10am for Mass; all other times by appointment. Bus: C22.

Palazzo Reale

This is Naples' most famous royal residence. Construction on the building began in 1600, taking two years to complete (although some finishing touches were still being added 50 years later). Designed by Neapolitan architect Domenico Fontana, the Royal Palace was constructed for the Spanish viceroys who dominated the city during much of the 17th century. One of the only residences in the city where original frescoes, paintings, furnishings and fixtures are still in their rightful place, the current interiors possess a neoclassical appearance, thanks largely to the French tastes of the 19th century, when entire wings were gutted at the pleasure of the Napoleonic rulers.

While the art collections are largely unimpressive, the **Teatrino di Corte** (a small, private theatre) and **Biblioteca Nazionale** (National Library) are worth a look. The library's collection of manuscripts and books is impressive, with some works dating back to the 5th century.

Access to the ticket office is badly marked. Look for the room to the left of the main entrance in order to get into the apartments located at the top of the staircase.
Piazza del Plebiscito 1. Tel: 081 580 8111; www.palazzorealenapoli.it. Open: Thur–Tue 9am–8pm; ticket office closes 1hr earlier. Admission charge. Bus: 24, C22, C82, R2, R3.

Palazzo Reale

Palazzo Serra di Cassano

This beautifully restored palazzo features a brilliant grey double stairway built out of the volcanic rock indigenous to the area. An individual appointment is the only way you can take a peek into the frescoed apartments, many of which feature original furniture. Today, the palazzo houses the Italian Institute for Philosophical Studies.
Via Monte di Dio 14. Tel: 081 245 2150; www.iisf.it. Open: by appointment. Bus: C22.

Walk: Via Toledo's faded grandeur

The history of Naples is one of permanent destruction and regeneration. As each period of fame and fortune fell by the wayside, residents shrugged off their problems, certain that the next period of good luck was sure to be just around the corner – at least in a few hundred years or so. In this walk we explore the grand palazzi of the Via Toledo, built during the boom years of the 18th century. They may have lost a bit of their lustre, but they'll never completely lose their looks.

This walk starts at the Galleria Umberto and takes approximately 2 hours.

1 Galleria Umberto

(*See p34 for details.*)

The complex runs from Piazza Trieste e Trento to Via Toledo. With your back to the Via Toledo exit, cross the road.

2 Palazzo Berio

This palazzo was designed by noted architect Luigi Vanvitelli, who is famous for also having designed the Villa Comunale and the Reggia in Caserta. The main square of Vomero is named after this favourite son of the city. Once noted for its extensive library and art collection, Palazzo Berio now houses collections by Benetton.

Via Toledo 256. Continue briefly up Via Toledo and cross the road again.

3 Palazzo Barbaja

Famous more for its residents than its design, this palazzo was the home of composer Gioacchino Rossini for seven years in the early 19th century.

Via Toledo 205. Cross Via Santa Brigida.

4 Palazzo Zevallos di Stigliano

A rare opportunity to enter one of the marvellous palaces on this route. The palazzo is now owned by Banca Intesa and this is its Naples gallery. The magnificent entrance portal into the lobby is the only original architectural feature, but you get a taste of the 19th-century good life as you wander through the interior. Come to see the bank's pride and joy: Caravaggio's *Martyrdom of Saint Ursula.*

Via Toledo 185. Open: Mon–Sat 10am–6pm. Tel: 800 160 52007; www.palazzozevallos.com. Admission charge.

5 Banco di Napoli

A prime example of imposing 1930s architecture favoured by the Fascist

regime. Think cold concrete, combined with athletic depictions of 'pure-blood' common people, and you get the idea.
Via Toledo 178.

6 Palazzo Buono

This was once one of the largest privately owned palazzi on the street, but underwent the ignominy of becoming a department store, its lovely interiors gutted.
Via Toledo 340.

7 Palazzo Carafa di Maddaloni

Further up the street on your right is this imposing palace, which takes its name from the Count of Maddaloni who first lived here. It was once one of the principal Baroque palaces of the city in terms of size, cost and style and the *piano nobile* was home to renowned artists of the day.
Via Toledo 26.

8 Palazzo Doria d'Angri

While you can't 'pull an Evita' by visiting the spot yourself, the balcony of this crumbling palazzo marks the location where Giuseppe Garibaldi declared the Unified Kingdom of Italy in September 1860. Note the pockmarks on the walls left from a World War II bomb that almost destroyed the building.
Via Toledo 29.

9 Piazza Dante

Restored to its former glory in 2002 to coincide with the metro station's grand opening, the piazza contains a statue of Dante staring sternly across Via Toledo. Behind the statue is the impressive crescent-shaped building known as the Convitto Nazionale, an ex-boarding school for impoverished kids. Children still fill the vast space, playing ball games or whizzing across the square on their bikes.
After Piazza Dante, Via Toledo becomes Via Enrico Pessina. Continue up the road.

10 Museo Nazionale Archeologico

(See pp58–9 for details.)
Piazza Museo 19. Tel: 081 442 2149; www.pompeiisites.org. Open: Museum Wed–Mon 9am–7.30pm. Gabinetto Segreto Wed–Mon 2.45–6.45pm. Tours 9.45am, 1.45pm. Admission charge.

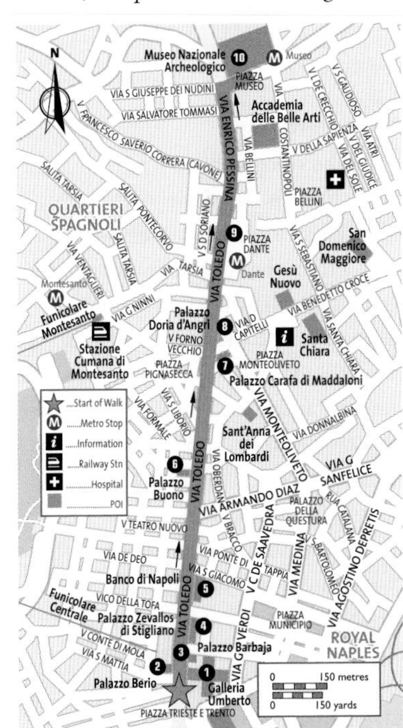

A statue at the Palazzo Reale depicts King Charles I of Naples

Parco Vergiliano

Amid the smog-choked streets of traffic lies this little jewel of greenery. To locate it, look under the railway bridge to the left of the church of Santa Maria di Piedigrotta. Climb the long staircase for a look into the **Crypta Neapolitana**, a 1st-century Roman road tunnel – and one of the world's longest. This engineering marvel originally connected Naples to the towns of Pozzuoli and Baia. Due to the precarious condition and old age of the crumbling tunnel, going inside is absolutely forbidden – you will have to make do with a view from above.

At the top of the staircase stands **Virgil's Tomb**. It is unknown whether or not the famed poet is actually buried in this large, beehive-shaped structure, but the tomb reads 'Mantua bore me, Calabria took me, Naples holds me'.

Salita della Grotta 20, Mergellina. Tel: 081 669 390. Open: daily 9am–1hr before sunset. Metro: Mergellina. Bus: C16, C24.

Piazza del Plebiscito

On hot summer weekends and New Year's Eve, this glorious public square is the site of music concerts, open-air theatre, buskers and political rallies. It's hard to believe that the restored volcanic cobblestones were covered in grime and the exhaust fumes of hundreds of inner-city buses as recently as 1994. Surrounding the piazza are Doric columns and a series of bronze equestrian statues dedicated to kings of the Bourbon dynasty.

Pizzofalcone

For beautiful views and a distinctive 'olde-worlde' buzz, the Pizzofalcone district is just the place. Two churches serve the community, **Santa Maria degli Angeli** and **Santa Egiziaca a Pizzofalcone**, but neither is of any specific significance. Santa Maria boasts a massive dome – and Santa Egiziaca is known for its unique convex façade.

San Francesco di Paola

An unpopular local church defaced by graffiti and pigeon detritus, the neoclassical design of San Francesco

is surprisingly rare in this city of Baroque ostentation. Its location on the Piazza del Plebiscito provides its doors with a stream of visitors drawn by its size and 53m (174ft)-high dome.
Piazza del Plebiscito.
Tel: 081 764 5133.
Open: Mon–Sat 7.30am–noon, 3.30–6pm, Sun 8.30am–12.30pm.
Bus: 24, C22, C82, R2, R3.

Santa Lucia

Featuring some of Naples' most picturesque back-alleys and hidden streets, the rambling fishermen's quarter of Pallonetto in Santa Lucia is a cosy corner of the city which is perfect for getting lost in. Filled with charming urban views, Santa Lucia has few tourist-geared sites that warrant a visit. Instead, enjoy a stroll along Via Chiatamone and Via Santa Lucia to take in the area's attractions.

Seafront

Castel dell'Ovo is reached by zigzagging your way down Mount Echia via the rambling **Rampa di Pizzofalcone**. From the bottom of the curving walkway, Via Partenope thrusts left towards the Santa Lucia fishermen's quarter and right to the five-star trappings of Chiaia. To find your way back to the Piazza del Plebiscito, follow Via Partenope along the seafront. The **Fontana dell'Immacolatella**, designed by Pietro Bernini and Michelangelo Naccherino, sits halfway along the route to the city centre.

Villa Comunale

Naples' green heart lies here along the edge of the Bay of Naples. Here is where countless Neapolitan couples have flirted and fallen in love, families come to picnic in the sunshine and pensioners choose to take their daily constitutional. Designed as a private park by Luigi Vanvitelli, it was originally used exclusively by the royal family – and it was opened just once a year to the general public on the feast of Mary's Nativity (8 September). Long rather than wide, its grounds follow the Chiaia coastline; however, it is separated from the peace and tranquillity of the lapping waves by the busy Via Francesco Caracciolo.
Riviera di Chiaia. Open: daily May–Oct 7am–midnight; Nov–Apr 7am–10pm. Bus: 140, 152, C28, R3. Tram: 1.

Piazza del Plebiscito

Walk: the birth of a city

Explore the earliest years of Naples in this walk, taking you from the sandy shores of the Bay of Naples to the city's royal seats of power.

The walk starts at the main entrance of the Gambrinus Café and takes approximately 3 hours.

1 Gambrinus Café

The watering hole of choice for the Neapolitan elite and their favoured artists, the Gambrinus has been dishing up mouthwatering cakes and positively passionate pastries for over a century. Its location near the doors of both the Teatro di San Carlo and the Galleria Umberto makes it the ideal post-shopping and pre-show location for either a quick coffee or a long gossip. Some of the rooms have only just been reopened after the Fascist leadership of the 1930s closed them down for their suspected links with left-wing politicians. Today, you are unlikely to spot any reds in the place unless seen as part of a motif in a Hermès headscarf. To get one of the better tables, be sure to dress as smartly as possible, making sure that all designer labels are coolly conspicuous. These waiters can sniff new money and/or a tourist better than a bloodhound!

Via Chiaia 1–2. Tel: 081 417 582; www.caffegambrinus.com. Open: daily 7am–1am.

Depart from the Gambrinus entrance for a guided tour of Acquedotto Carmignano.

2 Acquedotto Carmignano

(See p32 for details.)

Via Chiaia 1–2 (Bar Gambrinus). Tel: 081 400 256; www.lanapolisotterranea.it. Tours: Thur 9pm, Sat 10am, noon, 6pm, Sun 10am, 11am, noon, 6pm.

Return to the Gambrinus and cross Piazza Trieste e Trento into Piazza del Plebiscito.

3 Piazza del Plebiscito

(See p38 for details.)

Cross the square to the Palazzo Reale.

4 Palazzo Reale

(See p35 for details.)

Piazza del Plebiscito 1. Tel: 081 580 8111; www.palazzorealenapoli.it. Open: Thur–Tue 9am–8pm; ticket office closes 1hr earlier. Admission charge.

Facing Piazza del Plebiscito, turn left down Via Cesario Console and immediately left. Cross the green space and Via Acton to reach your next stop.

5 Giardini Pubblici

On weekends and pleasant evenings, this small park is filled with excitable groups hoping to practise their flirtation skills with members of the opposite sex. The views of the Bay are quite special, and it's a nice place to enjoy a quick drink or picnic lunch if you are so inclined – many others are.

With your back to the gardens, cross Via Acton and Via Cesario Console and go left until Via Santa Lucia.

6 Santa Lucia

This maze-like quarter has been home to the fishermen of the city for countless generations. Getting lost in these streets is a treat, especially if you enjoy watching everyday Neapolitan street life and the people who take part in it. If you like fresh fish, then a meal at any of the restaurants in the area is highly recommended.

Continue along Via Santa Lucia. At the end of the street lies Via Partenope. Turn right and cross the road to reach the final stop on the itinerary.

7 Castel dell'Ovo

The name of the 'Egg Castle' can be traced to a legend concerning the Roman poet Virgil, who it was believed in medieval times was a powerful magician. It was said he placed a magical egg in the castle's foundations to protect the city. (*See p33 for details.*)

Via Partenope. Tel: 081 240 0055. Open: Mon–Sat 8am–7.30pm, Sun 8am–2pm.

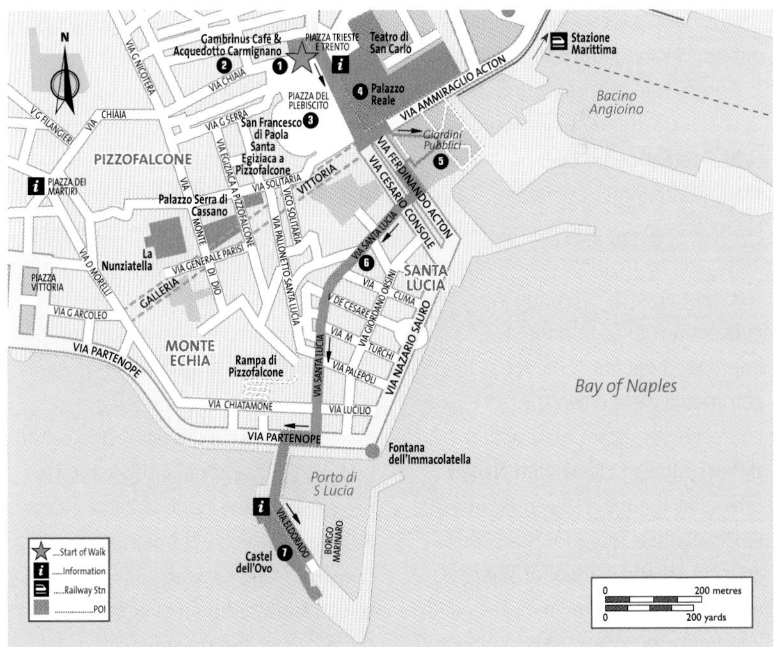

San Carlo and *commedia dell'arte*

Neapolitans have always loved their theatre – perhaps because their everyday life often resembles a life-size stage. Dramatic origins date back to the time of Nero when the fanciful emperor would take himself off to catch some of the ribald Roman comedies of the day. The popular Neapolitan theatrical form of *commedia dell'arte* can trace its origins back to this early form of entertainment in that both the early Roman theatre and *commedia* are based around stock characters and the use of masks which indicate differences in identity and emotion.

Commedia dell'arte found its feet in the 16th century when Renaissance tastes demanded a new outlet for their entertainment pleasure. Neapolitan mask and acting traditions were revived by the local acting trade, resulting in wild, eye-boggling concoctions of scripted and improvised delight. Characters in *commedia* were given the characteristics associated with different Italian cities, with Naples providing the much-loved figures of Pulcinella (the foul-mouthed, white-clad clown and symbol of the city) and Scaramouche (a Spanish captain known for his constant bragging and

The interior of the Teatro di San Carlo

cowardice). Pulcinella figurines are one of the most popular souvenirs brought home by visitors to the city. You'll spot the tiny statues depicting the cunning and mischievous scamp at almost every purveyor of tourist tat. Just look for the whimsical figure dressed in a white smock and trousers with a white dunce's cap for a hat and red-and-yellow-striped shoes.

If you're very lucky, there may even be a performance of *commedia* at Naples' most famous venue for the performing arts, the Teatro di San Carlo (although its dedication towards dance and opera makes this an extremely rare occurrence). Originally built in 1737 and rebuilt following a fire in 1816, San Carlo is Italy's oldest theatre and second in prominence only to Milan's La Scala. Shoestring budgets always loom over the producers of the theatre, with foreclosure a seemingly ever-present threat to the Teatro di San Carlo's ongoing survival, yet somehow the show always manages to go on – and the results are invariably stunning.

Openings at the San Carlo bring out the city's glitterati and are always the high point of the city's social calendar. While programming remains somewhat traditional, in the last couple of seasons attempts have been made to invigorate staging through the use of prominent visual artists such as David Hockney, or up-and-coming young directors.

The opera season runs throughout the year, with a two-month stoppage during the summer months because of the hot weather – there is no air-conditioning anywhere inside the venue. A subscription ticketing system means that seats for all performances are difficult to come by. If you go to the box office on the off-chance of buying a couple of tickets, you will probably be presented with the option of purchasing the worst seats in the house – the staff aren't being vindictive, they just don't have anything else they can sell you.

As for attire, think smart-casual. You won't find black-tie in the audience (with the exception of opening night); however, jeans and T-shirts will draw evil glares from the well-heeled crowds around you. Guided tours of the building are available, in the event that you can't score an elusive pair of tickets.
Teatro di San Carlo, Via San Carlo 98F. Tel: 081 797 2331; www.teatrosancarlo.it. Open: Box Office Tue–Sun 10am–7pm. Performance times and dates vary. Charge for tickets and tours. Bus: 24, C22, C25, C57, R2, R3.

The exterior of the Teatro di San Carlo

Walk: a seafront stroll

This walk along the Bay of Naples is a favourite for locals on a sunny Sunday afternoon. You can spot the remains of pine-wooded hills and fragrant backdrops that intoxicated visitors here in the 19th century during the era of the Grand European Tour. Follow in the footsteps of travellers on this walk, taking you from the heart of the city into idyllic Mergellina and the western suburbs.

Beginning at the grandstand in the Villa Comunale, this walk takes 2 hours to complete.

1 Villa Comunale

(*See p39 for details.*)
Riviera di Chiaia. Open: daily May–Oct 7am–midnight; Nov–Apr 7am–10pm.

2 Stazione Zoologica (Acquario)

Situated in the centre of the Villa Comunale, the Stazione Zoologica is a marine research organisation and one of Europe's oldest aquariums, founded in 1872 by German naturalist Anton Dohrn. The original 24 tanks, lined with volcanic rock and lit by skylights in the roof, still stand, calling themselves home to a number of local aquatic species, including octopuses, lobsters, seahorses and various fish. Legend has it that the liberating forces of 1944 held a victory banquet in the aquarium featuring a menu of its entire edible population. Today's custodians are more benign; the aquarium now provides a temporary shelter for many distressed animals found by the coast guard.
Acquario. Tel: 081 583 3263.
Open: Mar–Oct Tue–Sat 9am–6pm, Sun 9.30am–7.30pm; Nov–Feb Tue–Sat 9am–5pm, Sun 9am–2pm.
Admission charge.
Cross the Riviera di Chiaia to reach your next stop, the Villa Pignatelli.

3 Villa Pignatelli

This 19th-century villa has a strong British connection. Ferdinand Acton, son of the British prime minister Sir John Acton, built this imposing residence complete with a beautiful English-style garden. Eventually purchased and remodelled by the Rothschild family, the villa and grounds fell into the hands of the Italian government in 1952. Inside are some fantastic porcelains, busts and landscapes, which are well worth exploring. Villa Pignatelli's crown jewel is the 17th-century painting of *St George* by Francesco Guarino, although this is by no means the only masterpiece worth checking out.
Riviera di Chiaia 200. Tel: 081 669 675.
Open: Wed–Mon 8.30am–2pm.
Admission charge.

Follow the Riviera until you reach the San Giuseppe church on your right.

4 San Giuseppe a Chiaia

One of the most interesting Baroque churches in Naples, San Giuseppe was originally a chapel for the Jesuits. When they were run out of town, the church became both a nautical school and a hospice for the blind. Particularly of note is the stuccoed vaulted ceiling.
Riviera di Chiaia. Open: Mon–Sat 8am–noon, 5–8pm, Sun 8am–noon.
Continue down Riviera di Chiaia and turn left into Piazza della Repubblica. Then turn right on to Via Francesco Caracciolo, taking the right-hand fork into Via Mergellina.

5 The Chalets

The bracing seafront road leads to Porto Sannazero, where you can charter boats, and the charming Chalets. These kiosks act as ice-cream parlours, bars and restaurants. It's a pricey, though quaint place to stop for a break and a bite.
Go straight up Via Mergellina, through Piazza Sannazero and up Salita Piedigrotta.

6 Santa Maria di Piedigrotta

Just before the railway bridge is this seemingly unprepossessing church. Once the focal point of an exciting song festival celebrated on the feast-day of Mary's Nativity (8 September), efforts are being made to bring back the musical tradition sometime in the near future.
Open: Mon–Sat 7am–noon, 5–8pm, Sun 7am–2pm, 5–8pm.

7 Parco Vergiliano

(See p38 for details.)
Salita della Grotta 20. Tel: 081 669 390. Open: daily 9am–1hr before sunset. (The nearest metro is the attractive art-nouveau Mergellina station.)

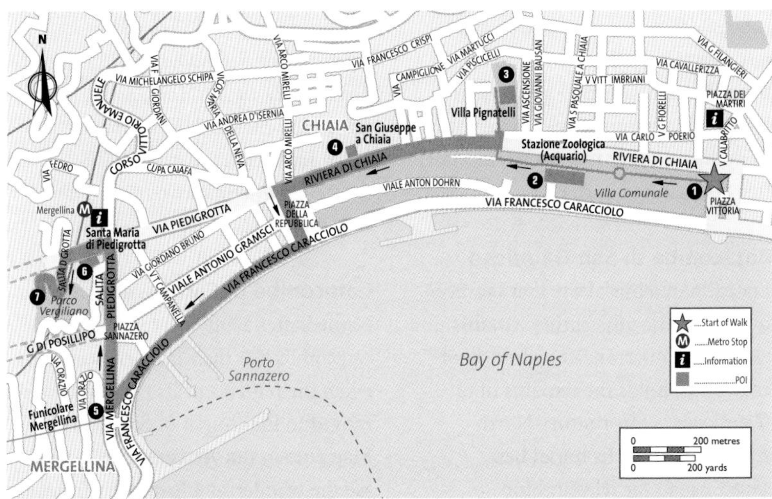

Naples: Centro Storico and La Sanità

The historic heart of the city, the Centro Storico is the district of Naples most visitors think of first. It is here that you will find the bulk of the city's oldest treasures, including the Duomo and the ancient Greek neighbourhood of Spaccanapoli. Geographically, the Centro Storico is tiny, yet its population density is among the highest in Europe.

Tiny streets and alleyways weave through the district, with precariously constructed buildings packed into every possible inch of space. A number of times throughout its history, the Centro Storico has come under threat from urban regeneration planners and health and safety operatives – it has also been host to a number of plagues throughout its precarious past. Today, the neighbourhood remains the rubbish-choked, overcrowded mess it has always been. Keep one eye on the beautiful sights around you and one eye on the ground to see where you're stepping, in order fully to appreciate this fascinating quarter.

Catacombe di San Gaudioso

Location of a burial site that has been used since the 5th century AD, this extensive subterranean collection of catacombs holds the remains of St Gaudiosus, a 5th-century North African bishop. His burial here transformed the labyrinthine, subterranean graveyard into an important shrine and place of holy pilgrimage. A variety of fascinating ancient burial practices is displayed and outlined by the competent tour guides, who lead you through the dark and musty caves that weave through the volcanic rock. Hour-long tours depart from the church of Santa Maria alla Sanità situated directly above the catacombs.

Via della Sanità 124. Tel: 081 544 1305; www.catacombedinapoli.it.
Tours: daily 10am, 11am, noon, 1pm. Admission charge. It is possible to buy a single ticket to enter all the catacombs. Metro: Cavour or Museo. Bus: C51, C52.

Catacombe di San Severo

Named after Saint Severus, these catacombs lost their importance when the remains of its namesake were moved to the church of San Giorgio Maggiore in the 9th century. Go to see the wonderful 4th-century frescoes

of St Peter and St Paul – the first representations of the apostles anywhere in the city.
Piazzetta San Severo a Capodimonte 81. Tel: 081 544 1305; www.catacombedinapoli.it. Open: Church daily 9.30am–12.30pm. Catacombs tours daily 10am, 11am, noon, 1pm. Metro: Cavour or Museo. Bus: C51, C52.

Centro Musei Scienze Naturali
A collection of four natural history museums owned and operated by Naples University. Subjects covered include geology, mineralogy, palaeontology, anthropology and zoology. The zoology museum is a particular favourite with children.
Via Mezzocannone 8. Tel: 081 253 7516; www.musei.unina.it. Open: Mon, Thur 9am–1.30pm, 3–5pm, Tue, Wed, Fri 9am–1.30pm, Sat, Sun 9am–1pm. Admission charge. Bus: 14, CD, E1, R2.

Cimitero delle Fontanelle
Closed to the public since the 1970s, this cemetery has an extremely grim

(*Cont. on p51*)

Skulls at the Cimitero delle Fontanelle

Walk: the Port and University

This walk starts and finishes at two bustling transport terminals: the main railway station and the port. Along the way, you'll slip into some quieter streets to get a taste of the real Naples and visit some significant historical sites. The walk starts at the main railway station (nearest metro: Garibaldi) and ends at the Port of Naples.

Allow 3 hours.

1 Stazione Centrale

This 1960s behemoth is undergoing a much-needed facelift. A place to people-watch, but keep an eye on your wallet.
Cross the square and the busy Via Alfonso d'Aragona. Proceed down Via P S Mancini, turn left into Via Capuana Maddalena and veer right into Via della Annunziata.

2 Santissima Annunziata

(*See p62 for details.*)
Turn right into Via Forcella.

3 The Forcella district

This area represents the stereotypes of Neapolitan life: racketeers, low-lifes and clan members have long roamed these mean streets. The Forcella district is one of poverty and strife, but it has a strong sense of community. As long as you don't flash your fancy jewellery or carry a costly camera, it's as safe as any other in the city.
From Via Forcella, turn left into Vicaria Vecchia and go straight on until you reach the church on your left.

4 San Giorgio Maggiore

This 17th-century church has a long history. The first basilica was built here in the 400s by Saint Severus, whose relics are housed behind the altar.
Turn left on to Via del Duomo.

5 Museo Filangieri

This striking 15th-century palace was demolished in the 1800s and moved to widen Via del Duomo. The museum houses a collection of weapons, armour and industrial and applied art.
Currently closed for restoration.
Turn right on to Via Arte della Lana, which runs into Via B Capasso.

6 Archivio di Stato

This State Archive was home to the convent of Santi Severino e Sossio.
Go straight on, past the Archive, and turn right on to Via G Paladino.

7 Università

Founded in 1224, Naples University is one of Europe's oldest. Its heart lies here just east of Piazza Bovio.

Turn left on to tiny Via G Orilia and take a left on Via Mezzocannone.

8 Centro Musei Scienze Naturali

(See p47 for details.)

Turn right into Via Sedile di Porto, then right on to Via G San Felice, then left into Via Medina and go straight on.

9 Fontana di Nettuno

Weirdly, Via Medina is both the original site and the new home of this 15th-century fountain of Neptune. Once removed to nearby Piazza Bovio, Neptune is back in its rightful place.

Continue down Via Medina on to Piazza Municipio and turn left.

10 Castel Nuovo

(See pp33–4 for details.)

Cross the traffic-congested Via Acton.

11 Port and Molo Beverello

It may not be pretty, but the port is for people-watching. Catch a boat from the Molo Beverello for a great view of the city – preferably at sunset.

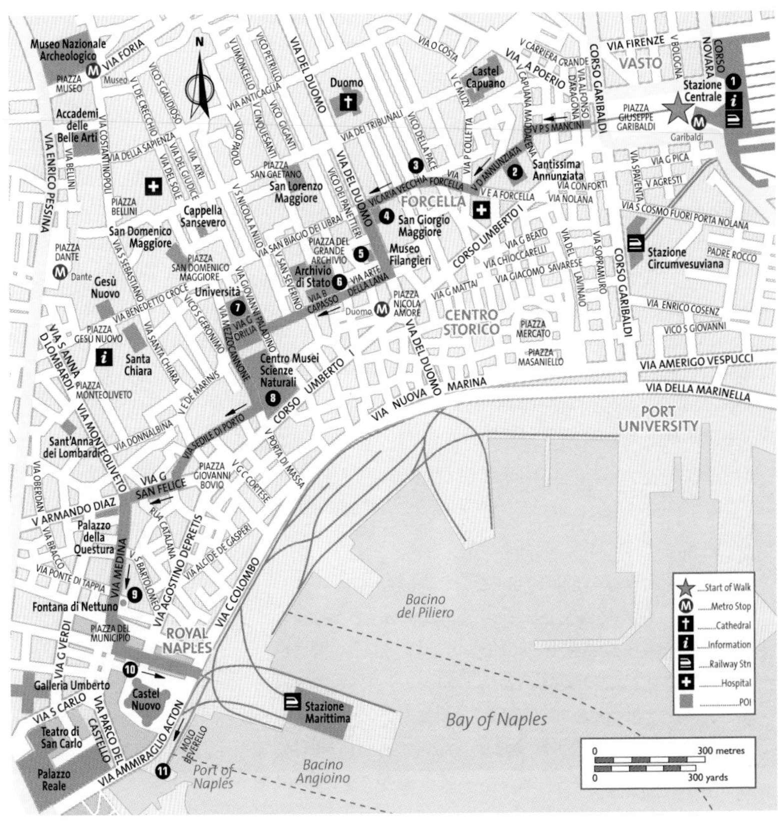

Interior of the Duomo

history, due to the number of dead transported here after the cholera epidemic of 1835. Eager to remove the diseased deceased from locations inside the city walls, hundreds of bodies were buried here in anonymous mass graves. When cholera reared its ugly head once again in 1973, more bodies were dumped in an effort to stem the tide of the disease. Over 40,000 skulls and bones are now stacked up throughout the massive cavern that makes up the structure. During World War II, 'skull worshipping' became a popular fad, as parents of children killed in action would adopt skulls in memory of their sons.

Via delle Fontanelle 154. Tel: 081 296 944. Closed indefinitely. Check with the Napoli Sotterranea society regarding potential reopening plans. Metro: Cavour or Museo. Bus: C51.

City walls

Until the mid-17th century, the city of Naples was firmly contained within its city walls. Unchanged for almost 2,000 years, the walls were considered essential by the Norman King Roger in 1140, yet proved to be a serious problem to future generations as the minute space within the walls stifled development and caused serious overcrowding. Little remains of the walls today, the best remaining stretch occurring at the **Porta Capuana** gate – a triumphal arch and series of towers dating back to 1484 and situated at the eastern end of Spaccanapoli.

Duomo

The main cathedral of Naples, the Duomo, can trace its history back to the 4th century. The current structure was built over what was once the church of Santa Stefania in the latter half of the 13th century. While the exterior fails to impress, the internal magnificence will be sure to take your breath away. Gilt covers almost every inch of the vaulted ceiling, while paintings by noted artist Luca Giordano, located between the various windows and arches, tell biblical stories and illuminate the figure of Christ.

The real draw is in the large chapel on the right. The **Cappella di San Gennaro** contains numerous artefacts, statues and busts dedicated to the patron saint of Naples, San Gennaro. Most of the really stunning items are only put on display during May and September in preparation for the days when San Gennaro's blood transforms into a liquid from its congealed state. During these sacred calendar dates, the Duomo holds a sea of worshippers, praying feverishly to bring luck (and liquid) to the auspicious occasion.

San Gennaro's skull bones and two phials of blood are kept in a 14th-century silver bust, which is locked permanently in a strongbox behind the altar.

Via Duomo 147. Tel: 081 449 097; www.duomodinapoli.com. Open: Church Mon–Sat 8am–12.30pm, 4.30–7pm,

(*Cont. on p56*)

Walk: Via dei Tribunali

On this walk, we discover Naples' contribution to Italian contemporary art. En route, there is liquefied blood, an underground shopping mall and a veiled Christ. If you intend to enter the places of worship mentioned, make sure to dress appropriately.

The walk starts on Via Settembrini (nearest metro: Cavour) and ends in Via Costantinopoli (nearest metro: Museo).

Allow 3 hours – more if you plan to linger in the MADRe.

1 MADRe

(*See pp56–7 for details.*)
Rightly considering itself a leader on the modern art scene, this museum is a showcase for what Naples has to offer the contemporary art world.
Leave the building and turn left, then immediately left on to Via Duomo. Continue to the Duomo on your left.

2 Duomo

(*See pp51 & 56 for details.*)
Enter Naples Cathedral and explore the large chapel on the right. It contains a number of artefacts dedicated to San Gennaro, including the famous blood.
Turn left out of the Duomo main doors and take a left at Via dei Tribunali.

3 Pio Monte della Misericordia

This chapel is part of a centuries-old charitable foundation and houses one of Naples' treasures: Caravaggio's *Seven Acts of Mercy*. The gallery behind the chapel contains paintings and furniture.
Via dei Tribunali 253.
www.piomontedellamisericordia.it.
Open: Church Mon–Sat 9.30am–1.30pm. Gallery Tue, Thur, Sat 9am–2pm.
Admission charge for gallery.
Retrace your footsteps to Via Duomo and continue along Via dei Tribunali.

4 San Lorenzo Maggiore

(*See p57 for details.*)
Via dei Tribunali is one of the three *decumani* (main roads) of Greek Neapolis. An incredible taste of ancient Naples lies here. Literally under your feet are the remains of a 2,000-year-old shopping area offering a wonderfully eerie view of life in ancient times.
Continue along Via dei Tribunali.

5 San Paolo Maggiore

This was originally the site of a Roman temple and the two pillars that stand in front of the church come from it. The church's crypt is dedicated to San Gaetano, whose statue adorns the eponymous square outside.
Return into Piazza San Gaetano.

6 Napoli Sotterranea

(*See p76 for details.*)

This is an opportunity to travel even further down into the bowels of the city. Not for the claustrophobic.

Piazza San Gaetano 68. www.napolisotterranea.org. Turn right into Via dei Tribunali and continue until Calata Severo. Turn left at the bottom of the street.

7 Cappella Sansevero

The reason we are here is to see the amazing *Cristo Velato* (*Veiled Christ*) by Giuseppe Sammartino. More ghoulish visitors might prefer the crypt, where embalmed figures loom in the gloom.

Retrace your steps to Via dei Tribunali, continuing left.

8 Piazza Bellini

This welcoming collection of cafés and bookstores in verdant surroundings is a popular haunt for aperitif tipplers and late-night romantics.

From Piazza Bellini turn right, going up Via Costantinopoli, which is full of antique stores.

9 Accademia delle Belle Arti

The Academy of Fine Arts façade is in the volcanic tufa stone and dates back to the mid-1800s. A hotbed of budding student talent, visitors should head for the Fine Art Gallery for a taste of contemporary art.

From here, you are a short walk from the Museo metro station, situated at the top of the street.

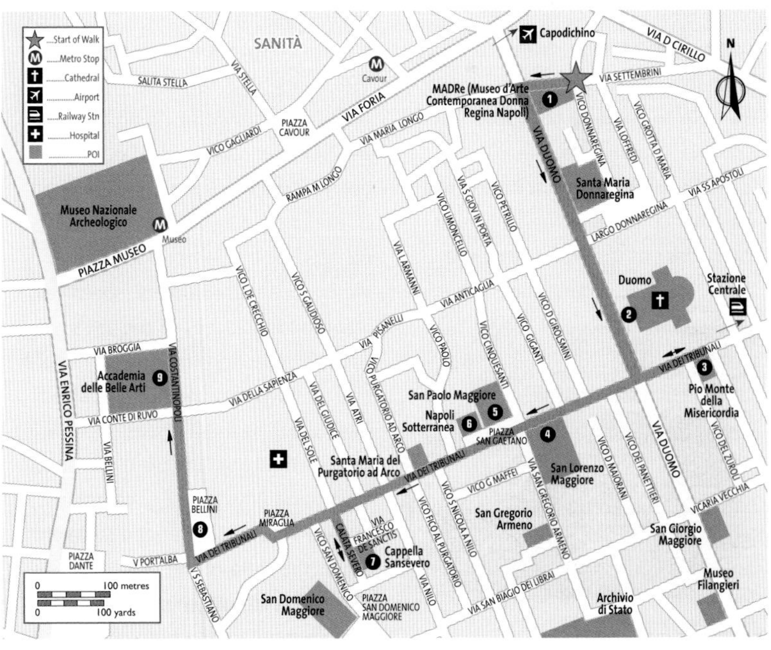

The *camorra* clans

The history of organised crime in Naples dates back centuries; however, the large-scale criminal activity associated with the crime-lords of today is a far cry from the relatively gentle smuggling and theft that made up the bulk of profits until the closing days of World War II. Known by the ancient Spanish name of *La camorra*, local mafia hoods were primarily involved in two-bit operations until the arrival of crime-boss Raffaele Cutolo during the mid-1970s. Up until then, organised crime units occupied themselves with profits made from cigarette, fruit and vegetable smuggling. Cutolo upped the ante by creating his *Nuova Camorra Organizzata*. Clans that failed to join his band of merry men were forced to join together under the banner of the *Nuova Famiglia Unita*. The two organisations have been battling between themselves for control of the city ever since. Cutolo is famous for soaking up millions of lire in reconstruction money following the earthquake of 1980, leaving thousands homeless and numerous housing projects unfinished as funds ran dry. Police did much to attack the *camorra* clans after evidence of their post-earthquake racketeering came to light, only to find that the groups fractured into a number of smaller-scale families willing to fight to the death for their pockets of neighbourhood control.

Patrolling the streets

The darkest years occurred between 1983 and 1993, when ten mayors in a row failed to do anything to crack the hold the *camorra* had on everything from basic public services to the street tobacco trade. Strikes dictated by the *camorra* leadership were a common problem, specifically involving employees of the city's rubbish collection companies. Rubbish and well-fed rats lined the crowded streets during these disease-ridden periods of action, crippling the police forces and any honest government leaders who might happen to care about the state of the city.

Property development and construction are the two industries

The *camorra* managed the street tobacco trade

in which the bulk of illegal profits have been made. Numerous poorly designed projects and buildings sprouted up throughout the chaotic post-war period, much to the chagrin (and secret financial delight) of city councillors. Despite the introduction of hundreds of building codes and laws designed to prevent an explosion in mismanaged architecture, local leaders often turned a blind eye as their wallets were lined with kickback money which was provided with the compliments of their friendly, neighbourhood criminal clans.

The year 1992 proved to be the end of the line for the gravy train, as the *Mani Pulite* (clean hands) campaign swept a number of corrupt practices and politicians out of office and into the criminal courts. However, now that local government is proving not to be above a bit of backhanding, the *camorra* is evolving yet again. Recent scams that keep the police busy include illegal prescription drug distribution, the sale of faulty second-hand airline parts and a complex con involving cloned southern Italian number plates, registration papers and insurance details sold to northern Italian drivers, thus enabling them to collect endless traffic and parking fines – only for the final bill to be sent to the unsuspecting southern car owner whose details had been forged originally.

The *camorra* is adept at transforming its criminal operation into service industries. The adage 'where there's muck there's brass' is particularly true of Naples and the *camorra*'s involvement in waste disposal management. They put legitimate businessmen at the helm of bogus waste disposal companies, then either don't collect the city's rubbish or dump it illegally outside the city causing environmental damage and pollution. As Naples gradually disappeared under tonnes of stinking waste, things came to a head in 2008 when protesters and police clashed. The army was brought in to bulldoze the waste, while firemen fought blazing rubbish heaps. Despite government intervention, the *camorra* still has a hand in this dirty business.

Cacti at Orto Botanico

Sun 8am–1.30pm, 5–7.30pm. Collections and baptistery Mon–Sat 9am–noon, 4.30–6.30pm, Sun 8.30am–1pm. Admission charge for collections and baptistery. Bus: E1, R2.

Gesù Nuovo

Originally a palazzo, this church is notable for its façade of raised, diamond-shaped stone. The interior was transformed from a place of residence to a place of worship in the 16th century by architect Giuseppe Valeriani. Of particular interest is a room dedicated to local saint Giuseppe Moscati, a 20th-century Neapolitan doctor who forsook the trappings of wealth and prestige in order to tend to the health of the local poor.
Piazza Gesù Nuovo 2. Tel: 081 557 8111. Open: daily 7am–12.30pm, 4–7.30pm. Free admission. Metro: Dante or Montesanto. Bus: E1, R1.

MADRe (Museo d'Arte Contemporanea Donna Regina Napoli)

Ever since the Neapolitan revival of 1994, Naples has been carving a name for itself as the capital of the modern

art scene. The opening of this gallery in the Centro Storico in 2005 finally cemented the city's position, with works by Damien Hirst, Jeff Koons and Francesco Clemente on permanent display. More gallery space, dining facilities and an outdoor courtyard were added in 2008.
Via Settembrini 79. Tel: 081 562 4561; www.museomadre.it. Open: Mon, Wed–Sun 10am–midnight. Admission charge; free on Sat. Metro: Cavour or Museo. Bus: 47, CS, E1.

Orto Botanico (Botanical Gardens)

Founded by Joseph Bonaparte in 1807, these gardens, while located in one of Naples' most crowded districts, are a haven of peace and tranquillity. The selection of trees and plants is serviceable, including a number of palms, ferns and aquatic shrubs. A *castello* in the centre of the park features museum displays dedicated to the world of botany and is now operated by the Naples University science department.
Via Foria 223. Tel: 081 449 759; www.ortobotanico.unina.it. Open: pre-booking only Mon–Fri 9am–2pm. Metro: Cavour or Museo. Bus: 14, 15, 47, CD, CS, C51.

San Lorenzo Maggiore

This extremely popular church was restored back to its original 13th-century form following extensive post-war renovation. While the façade makes the church look decidedly Baroque in construction, this is merely a superficial addition to the original Gothic design – a change made to reflect the tastes of the period and the Neapolitan love affair with anything ostentatious. Readers of Naples' answer to *The Canterbury Tales*, the *Decameron*, should note that it was within these church walls that Boccaccio fell in love with Fiammetta. Be sure not to miss the original mosaic flooring preserved under glass in the transept.
Via dei Tribunali 316. Tel: 081 211 0860; www.sanlorenzomaggiorenapoli.it. Open: Mon–Sat 9.30am–5pm, Sun 9.30am–1pm. Free admission to church. Metro: Dante or Montesanto. Bus: E1.

Tower of San Lorenzo Maggiore

The Museo Nazionale Archeologico

Paris has the Louvre. Madrid boasts the Prado. And London has the British Museum. For Naples, the crown jewel of museums must be the Museo Nazionale Archeologico. Home to one of the world's largest collections of Roman and ancient artefacts, the museum holds many treasures excavated from the digs of Herculaneum, Pompeii and Stabiae, as well as numerous other must-sees drawn from the sea-based empires of the Mediterranean that once ruled the world.

Formerly home to Naples University, King Ferdinand I transformed this massive four-storey palazzo into a museum after inheriting a number of ancient pieces from his grandmother. Following the discovery of Pompeii, the rooms filled up fast. Today's museum only exhibits a fraction of what is actually owned. Collections include a vast selection of Egyptian objects, many of which were transported to Italy and unearthed in digs in the Campania region, an excess of Greek busts and statuary, intricate mosaics and a scandalous room of ancient pornography.

Reopened in 2000, the decidedly soft-core Gabinetto Segreto (Secret Cabinet) boasts a number of blush-inducing images, including a range of phallic talismans, a collection of erect Pan sculptures and explicit paintings and mosaics removed from the private bedrooms of some of Pompeii's richest citizens. Note that this collection is off limits to anyone under the age of 11

Museo Nazionale Archeologico

and is watched by a small gaggle of female attendants at all times.

The bulk of the treasures plundered from Herculaneum and Pompeii can be found on the first floor of the museum, centred on the Sala Meridiana. This may change at any moment, however, as constant upkeep and renovation keep the rooms moving around, depending upon construction schedules. From the Sala, the first few rooms you pass through hold silverware, pottery, glassware and other decorative and everyday household objects. In Rooms 114 to 117, just before the entrance to the Sala, all the artefacts are from the Villa dei Papiri in Herculaneum. Vases, bowls and urns can be found in the second set of rooms on the right. All of these objects are from sites further afield in southern Italy.

A large collection of Palaeolithic, Neolithic and Bronze Age items, dating back to 100,000 BC, is located along the third corridor on the right from the Sala Meridiana. Stone flints and funerary offerings are arranged in location order, with the best finds coming from the necropolis of Capri. If busts and statues are your passion, stick to the ground floor's Farnese collection. The powerful Farnese family pilfered a ton of treasures from ancient sites in Rome during the 16th century. Pope Paul III, otherwise known as Alessandro Farnese, filtered many of the Church's ancient holdings into the hands of his influential clan.

Mosaic from the collection

While the Farnese paintings are holed up in the Capodimonte museum just up the street, the heavier marble items featuring characters from Greek and Roman legend and society can be found in the rooms just off the main open-air heart of the museum, directly in front of the main entrance.

Modern and visiting exhibits are another factor in museum geography, with big-name shows usually housed in the vast rooms on the ground floor, to the right of the ticket office.

Museo Nazionale Archeologico, Piazza Museo 19. Tel: 081 442 2149; www.pompeiisites.org. Open: Museum Wed–Mon 9am–7.30pm; ticket office closes 1hr earlier. Gabinetto Segreto Wed–Mon 2.45–6.45pm. Tours 9.45am, 1.45pm. Admission charge.
Metro: Museo or Cavour. Bus: 47, CS, E1.

The courtyard of Santa Chiara

Sant'Anna dei Lombardi

The most notable Renaissance church in a city not known for its Renaissance architecture, this church is worth including on your itinerary, in order to examine the unique inlaid wooden panels that line the walls and the collection of terracotta statues by Guido Mazzoni entitled *Mourning the Death of Christ.*

Piazza Monteoliveto 44.
Tel: 081 551 3333. Open: Tue–Fri 8.30am–noon, Sat 8.30am–noon, 5.30–6.30pm. Free admission. Metro: Montesanto. Bus: E1, R1, R4.

Santa Chiara

This Gothic church was built during the reign of Robert of Anjou. Bomb attacks and Baroque reconstruction did much to reduce this place of worship favoured by the aristocracy – following World War II, all that was left were the four church walls.

Go past the cloister for a look at salvaged pieces from the original 14th-century structure, shards of bomb shrapnel and excavations below the surface that reveal a gymnasium and baths from the age of the Roman Empire.
Via Benedetto Croce. Tel: Church 081 797 1235, Museum 081 551 6673; www.monasterodisantachiara.eu. Open: Church daily 7.30am–1pm, 4.30–8pm. Museum and cloister Mon–Sat 10am–2.30pm, Sun 9.30am–1pm. Admission charge to enter museum and cloister. Metro: Dante or Montesanto. Bus: E1.

Santa Maria del Purgatorio ad Arco

A decidedly eerie church – and one that has captured the imaginations of the thoroughly superstitious Neapolitan population – Santa Maria del Purgatorio ad Arco is also known as the 'death's head' church, on account of the three bronze skulls that sit outside its railings. During periods of famine, plague and war, Neapolitan women adopted skulls and cared for them in place of loved and lost menfolk. Today, adopted skulls are used to request divine favours and intercession. While this tradition is banned as idolatrous by the Catholic Church, the practice is said to live on.
Currently closed for restoration. Call ahead for information.
Via dei Tribunali 39. Tel: 081 292 622. Open: daily 9am–1pm. Free admission to church. Metro: Dante or Montesanto. Bus: E1.

Santa Maria Donnaregina

The condition of Santa Maria Donnaregina owes much to the fact that it was decidedly out of favour and abandoned for 250 years from the 1600s to the 1850s. Due to the public preference for the 17th-century church located right next door, Santa Maria's frescoes, interiors and Gothic architecture were left untouched – the result is one of Naples' most authentic churches.
Vico Donnaregina 26.
Tel/Fax: 081 299 101. Open: by appointment. Bus: E1.

Santissima Annunziata

The Annunziata complex of fountains, courtyards and an adjoining orphanage dates back to the 14th century; however, the church owes its appearance to the designs of Vanvitelli (famous for his Reggia in Caserta). Details to note are the fine majolica clock that dominates the bell tower over the entrance, the 16th-century wooden doors, and a foundling wheel that was still in use until the 1980s. Unwanted children would be placed in the foundling wheel for acceptance by the orphanage directors, with abandoned children given the name Esposito (meaning 'laid before God's mercy'). You may notice locals avoid the foundling wheel at all costs. Many still associate its presence with hard times when unwanted and unaffordable pregnancies resulted in starvation and stigma.
Via dell'Annunziata 34.
Tel: 081 283 017;
www.annunziatamaggiore.it.
Open: Wheel Mon–Sat 9am–6pm.
Church Mon–Sat 8am–noon, 5–7.30pm, Sun 8am–1.30pm. Free admission.
Metro: Garibaldi. Bus: R2. Tram: 1.

Spaccanapoli

The original Greek and Roman heart of the city, this is where the city of Neapolis took form to become the metropolis of today. Spaccanapoli is not so much an area as it is a name for the ancient *decumanus inferior* – a series of streets that made up the centre of Naples. If today's planners were as smart as the first Greeks, then the city would be planned on a grid system just like it was in times of old. The bulk of Spaccanapoli is now pedestrianised, although you will often find a number of cheeky scooter-drivers making a break for it when the city becomes too clogged to move through. The shops that line the streets follow ancient patterns: around the university you will find a number of bookshops, stationery shops and purveyors of musical instruments – many of which have existed in the same location for generations (*see walk on pp64–5*). Religious artefact shops, pricey jewellers and souvenir stores are usually located near churches and other tourist hot spots.

Via San Gregorio Armeno

Housing a fine collection of souvenir shops, this delicate street runs downhill from the Via dei Tribunali towards the State Archives. The savvy shopkeepers of San Gregorio know that their salaries are in the hands of the tourists, so lunch-hour closures are uncommon. Everything from Pulcinella figurines to light-up Nativity crèches is available for sale, albeit at a vastly inflated price. An abundance of striped awnings makes shopping a possibility on even the most rain-choked of days. Good for browsing and the occasional impulse purchase.

The columns of San Paolo Maggiore

Walk: Spaccanapoli

This walk cuts a swathe across the city from the infamous Quartieri Spagnoli, heaving with the local populace, taking you along streets bursting with tourists. Amid the chaos lie some of the city's loveliest buildings, with a few offering a peaceful haven from the hustle and bustle.

The walk starts at the metro station of Montesanto and ends in Via dei Tribunali.

Allow 2 hours.

1 Quartieri Spagnoli

Taking its name from Spanish troops who occupied it in the 16th century, the poorest inhabitants of the city turned the area into slums once the invaders had left. But what the area lacks in grandeur it makes up for in energy and ambience.

From the station, head southeast down Via Porta Medina, reaching Piazza Pignasecca. Continue down Via Forno Vecchio, crossing Via Toledo into Via D Capitelli. Go straight on.

2 Gesù Nuovo

(*See p56 for details.*)

Not only is the church amazing, there's also a towering obelisk in the square (plus a tourist information centre). Don't forget to look at the *ex-votos* to saintly doctor Giuseppe Moscati.

With the main entrance behind you, turn left until you reach the entrance to Santa Chiara on your right.

3 Santa Chiara

(*See p61 for details.*)

This quiet corner offers a history lesson spanning over 2,000 years, but it also gives you an opportunity to put your feet up in the restful atmosphere.

With the church façade behind you, turn right and walk to the crossroads.

4 Via San Sebastiano

The road running north to south is Via San Sebastiano to your left and Via Santa Chiara to your right. To your left is the tiny Church of Santa Marta. Its cemetery contains the remains of dozens of boy soldiers, killed in the Masaniello uprising of 1647.

Cross Via San Sebastiano into Via Benedetto Croce.

5 Via Benedetto Croce

Named after the city's philosopher and historian, there are great shops and even greater palaces, including Croce's own home at Palazzo Filomarino.

Continue down Via Benedetto Croce.

6 San Domenico Maggiore

From the pretty piazza this building looks more like a castle than a church. Inside there is art dating back to the 1200s, as well as a ghoulish array of coffins in the sacristy.

Piazza San Domenico Maggiore 8A. Open: daily 8.30am–noon, 4.30–7pm.

Continue down Via Benedetto Croce to Piazzetta Nilo.

7 Sant'Angelo a Nilo

This charming little church houses the only Donatello in Naples. Founded early in the 15th century, the name Nilo (Nile) derives from the Alexandrians who lived in this area 2,000 years ago.

Piazzetta Nilo. Open: Mon–Sat 9am–noon, 4–6pm, Sun 9am–noon.

Continue down the street, which turns into Via San Biagio dei Librai. Turn left on to Via San Gregorio Armeno.

8 Via San Gregorio Armeno

(See p62 for details.)

A great place to pick up a souvenir or Nativity piece.

9 San Gregorio Armeno

The cloisters contain orange trees and a fountain. Sit here for a while to soak up the calm atmosphere before heading back out into the chaos.

Via San Gregorio Armeno 1. Open: Mon, Wed–Fri 9am–noon, Tue 9am–12.45pm, Sat & Sun 9am–12.30pm.

Continue down Via San Biagio dei Librai to Via Duomo, turning right to reach the Duomo metro station.

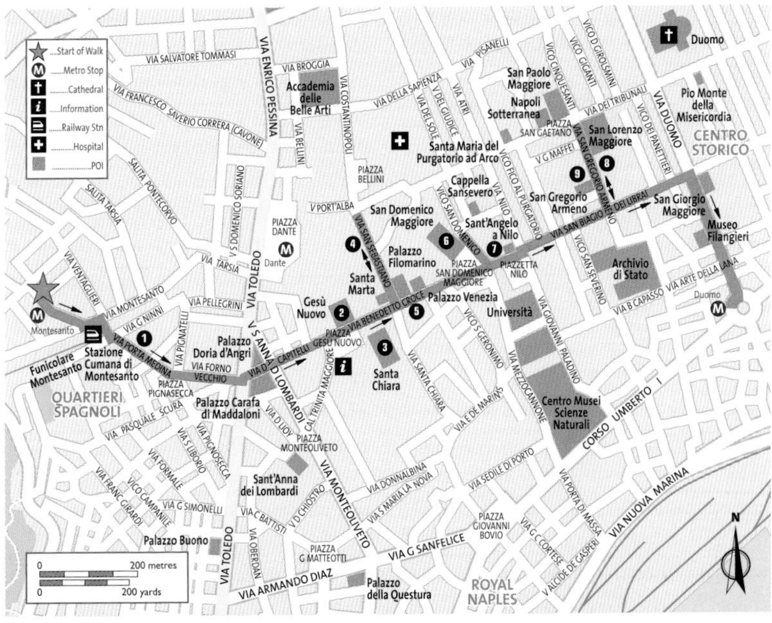

Naples: Vomero

Before World War II, Vomero was seen as a small, countrified suburb of sprawling Naples. Families would take the funicular up the hillside past the numerous farms (the district officially had a higher population of sheep than it did of people) and enjoy picnics in the cool air of the Castel Sant'Elmo.

With post-war reconstruction came post-war gloom as unscrupulous property speculators transformed the district into a sea of middle-class high-rise developments almost overnight. For years afterwards, Vomero was seen as the worst neighbourhood in Naples in terms of traffic chaos. With only four funicular lines running every ten minutes between Vomero and the city centre, commuting was a mess. Only with the introduction of the underground station and new metro lines has any headway even started to be made in what was essentially Europe's largest permanent car park.

Castel Sant'Elmo

The Castel Sant'Elmo boasts what are probably Naples' most glorious views. While not the original structure, the current building owes much of its look to additions made in the 16th century when it gained its six-pointed star shape. A castle has existed at this strategic location overlooking the Bay of Naples since 1329, when King Robert of Anjou constructed a fortification above a small church dedicated to St Erasmus, or 'Elmo' – hence the name.

A walk through the castle can be strangely spooky, especially during the gloomy winter months. A spacious modern and experimental art collection takes up many of the interior spaces, including the dungeons on the first floor – some of which were still being used for military prisoners until as recently as the 1970s. The top floor, otherwise known as the **Piazza d'Armi**, acts as the roof of the castle, from which you can obtain breathtaking views of the city below.

Via Tito Angelini 22. Tel: 081 578 4030; www.napolibeniculturali.it. Open: Wed–Mon 9am–7.30pm. Admission charge. Funicular: Montesanto to Via Morghen, Centrale to Piazzetta Fuga or Chiaia to Via Cimarosa. Bus: V1.

Certosa-Museo di San Martino

The Museo di San Martino boasts one of the most intriguing collections of treasures in the city. To its credit, San Martino is more than just a museum. A former monastery, the grounds of the Certosa-Museo hold an art gallery, a collection of Nativity scenes and a spectacular church, in addition to the aforementioned museum. The highlight of the collection is the fascinating *Tavola Strozzi* – a 3-D depiction of the city of Naples as it looked in the 15th century. Familiar buildings, including the Castel Nuovo and the Certosa, can be seen if you look hard enough.

Piazzale San Martino 5.
Tel: 081 229 4502. Open: Thur–Tue 8.30am–7.30pm; ticket office closes 1hr earlier. Admission charge.
Funicular: Montesanto to Via Morghen, Centrale to Piazzetta Fuga or Chiaia to Via Cimarosa. Bus: V1.

Corso Vittorio Emanuele

Each district of Naples has its 'main street' and Vomero is no exception. Corso Vittorio Emanuele wraps around the length of Vomero, separating it from the streets of the city centre below. In certain sections, it's decidedly

(*Cont. on p70*)

Glorious views of Naples from the Castel Sant'Elmo

Funiculì, Funiculà

In 1889, the district of Vomero became a viable residential quarter, thanks largely to the invention of a pair of local engineers, Bruno and Ferraro. These two canny industrial pioneers designed a funicular rail system that allowed passengers to ascend the precarious sides of Vomero hill along the Chiaia and Montesanto slopes. The 'train of delights', as it was called, passed up the rural hillside to the top of Vomero, finally stopping to allow passengers a stunning view of the bay. In those days Vomero was known for its vineyards and farmlands – not for the upmarket apartment blocks of today. Following its successful inclusion into the Neapolitan transport network, locals flocked to the cooler breezes, ample space and altogether more pleasant air of Vomero, transforming it almost overnight into one of the city's most popular middle-class residential neighbourhoods.

In total, four lines run between Vomero and the districts below: the Chiaia line (1889), Montesanto (1891), the Mergellina and the Centrale (1928). The longest funicular of the four, the Centrale, begins its journey in Via Toledo, reaching a point near the Via Scarlatti halfway between the Chiaia and Montesanto lines. For direct access to the seafront and the western suburbs, the Mergellina funicular, running from Via Manzoni, is the best option.

Rides on the funicular proved to be so popular that a famous song was composed in the late 19th century, broadcasting its reputation. *Funiculì*, *Funiculà* can still be heard on many recordings today, especially in the streets of the city that sparked the craze.

As only two trains run on the railway system at any given time (one up and one down), rides can get exceedingly busy during the traditional morning and evening rush hours. It's best to avoid this time of day unless you like the idea of being jammed into the corner of a sweaty train-car leaning on a steep incline. Due to the popularity of casual rides, the usual 90-minute ticket is only useable once on the funicular system.

Before the advent of the funicular age, travellers to Vomero were forced to traverse a long flight of steps leading up from the city centre. By day, these steps make for an enjoyable journey, especially if you want to avoid the chaotic traffic that plagues the city. By night, its location makes it a prime target for muggings and petty theft. Be alert if you take the risk.

Another funicular railway built by the dynamic design duo of Bruno and Ferraro was a precarious track up the sides of Vesuvius. Erected in 1880, this funicular, consisting of just two cars, took visitors up to an altitude of 1,180m (3,870ft) above sea level. A number of accidents plagued the system for the duration of its all-too-brief lifetime, finally forcing the Vesuvius funicular to close in 1944.

Tickets can be bought at any of the funicular railway stations. Tel: 800 568 866. www.metro.na.it. Trains run every 10, 12 or 15 minutes. Funiculare Centrale: from city centre to the Villa Floridiana. Open: daily 6.30am–12.30am. Funiculare di Chiaia: from Via del Parco Margherita to the Villa Floridiana. Open: daily 6.30am–12.30am. Funiculare di Montesanto: Cumana station to the Castel Sant'Elmo and Via Scarlatti. Open: daily 7am–10pm. Funiculare di Mergellina: from Via Mergellina to Via Manzoni. Open: daily 7am–10pm.

Funicular rides are very popular in Naples

ugly. However, the bulk of Naples' luxury hotel options are situated along this avenue on the border with Chiaia. Why Vomero? you might ask. The answer is the views. Clinging precariously to the hillside above, residents of this tiny stretch of land enjoy the cooling breezes that come with living halfway up the inner city's highest point in addition to some of the most stunningly unobstructed views of the Bay of Naples below. If you don't fancy traipsing down this long road, catch a C27 bus, which will whizz you along the panoramic route. A drink at the **Grand Hotel Parker's** (*Corso Vittorio Emanuele 135*), while enjoying the sunset, was almost a rite of passage for 'Grand Tour' British tourists during the peak of 19th-century travel to the city.

Vista over Naples and Vesuvius from the Castel Sant'Elmo

Museo Nazionale della Ceramica Duca di Martina

The world of ceramics is celebrated in this museum. The first floor is dedicated to the history of European work, including pieces from Meissen and obligatory examples of fine Capodimonte figurines. The ground floor holds international work, with a focus on Japanese and Chinese pieces. *Via Cimarosa 77. Tel: 081 578 8418. Open: Wed–Mon 9am–2pm. Admission charge. Funicular: Montesanto to Via Morghen, Centrale to Piazzetta Fuga or Chiaia to Via Cimarosa. Bus: E4, V1.*

Parco della Floridiana

If the tree-lined avenue of Via Scarlatti doesn't calm your nerves, then this favoured park most probably will. Built as a wedding gift for the Duchess of Floridiana by her husband King Ferdinand, the gardens and villa were opened to the public in the 1920s after they were purchased by the state. Since that time, the system of paths and intimate benches has made it one of the best spots for a quiet stroll in the city. *Via Cimarosa 77. Tel: 081 578 8418. Open: Park daily 8.30am–1hr before sunset. Funicular: Montesanto to Via Morghen, Centrale to Piazzetta Fuga or Chiaia to Via Cimarosa. Bus: E4, V1.*

Via Scarlatti

At the heart of the community lies Via Scarlatti – recently pedestrianised in order to promote the new car-free community Vomero is so desperately trying to promote. Café tables pour out onto this elegant tree-lined avenue, bringing out thousands of locals on warm summer nights. A stroll down here rivals that even of glamorous Via Toledo among the upper classes of Neapolitan society. The focal point of Via Scarlatti is Piazza Vanvitelli, named after the local architect who made his name designing such structures as the Villa Comunale and the Reggia in Caserta.

Cimarosa Station

Naples: Capodimonte

Visit the glorious hillside heaven of Capodimonte if you're a fan of breathtaking museums, lush gardens, vivid views and other tantalising touristy treats perfect for those days when you're lazy or just plain worn out.

On a clear day you can see for miles from the balconies of the Palazzo Reale di Capodimonte – built for King Charles III in the 18th century. Before the construction of this massive pile, Capodimonte was a generally disregarded hill located far outside the city walls. But it was the king's passion for sport that changed all of that. This verdant retreat provided top-class hunting grounds, perfect for those typically overcast Neapolitan days when there was just nothing for a king to do.

A Garden of Eden

While it's not even a quarter of the size of Europe's grandest green spaces (Bois de Boulogne, Hyde Park, Tiergarten), the park surrounding the **Museo di Capodimonte** can lay claim to being one of the best on the continent. Designed in the 18th century by Ferdinand Sanfelice, the park has five avenues radiating from the palace like spokes on a wheel.

Museo di Capodimonte: Porta Grande, Via Capodimonte.
Tel: 081 749 9111;
www.napolibeniculturali.it.
Open: Tue–Sat 10am–7pm, Sun 9am–2pm. Admission charge.

What lies beneath

The rest of the sights of Capodimonte are downhill from here – literally.

A quiet street in Capodimonte

Titian's *Danae* at the Museo di Capodimonte

Directly below the palazzo lie the remains of what was once the most important point of pilgrimage in the city of Naples. The **Catacombe di San Gennaro** (*see below*) once held relics of the city's patron saint, San Gennaro. When his remains and phials of his blood were moved to the Duomo, the catacombs lost their page in Neapolitan history books.

ALL WALLED OUT

There must be more than one way around a set of city walls. At least that's what Byzantine General Belisarius had to figure out during his siege of Naples in AD 536. Deciding to avoid the futility of a direct attack, the knowledgeable general used the city's defences against them by sneaking through the **Ponti Rossi** aqueduct. This fresh-water supplier, built by the Emperor Claudius in the 1st century, provided direct access into the heart of the city centre. You can still see the well-preserved ruins of the aqueduct leading down from Capodimonte's **Porta Grande**. Not only was the general victorious, he also managed to avoid an almost-certain watery grave.

Catacombe di San Gennaro

Lucky San Gennaro. Not only does he have a city in his thrall over two phials of his blood, he also gets to commune

with the dead in a catacomb named after him. Two levels of catacombs contain some much-muddied frescoes dating as far back as the 2nd century AD. But it wasn't until the body of San Gennaro was brought here in the 5th century that the catacombs became a place of pilgrimage and religious worship.
Via Capodimonte 16. Tel: 081 544 1305; www.catacombedinapoli.it.
Tours: daily 10am, 11am, noon, 1pm; Easter–Nov also 2pm, 3pm, 4pm, 5pm. Group tours available by appointment only. Admission charge. Bus: 24, 110, R4.

Museo di Capodimonte

Naples' 'other' great art collection, the Museo di Capodimonte, is the sister museum to the Museo Nazionale in that it holds the great paintings of the celebrated Farnese collection. Many would argue that Capodimonte got the better pieces to showcase, including a number by Raphael and Titian. The climax of the first floor is Titian's *Danae*, located in Room 11. Painted for the sleeping chambers of a Cardinal, this ambitious masterpiece is surprisingly erotic, portraying the naked Danae seduced by Jupiter. Other big names featured at the Capodimonte include Botticelli, El Greco, Renoir, Caravaggio, Rembrandt, Tintoretto and a couple of fine Brueghels.
Porta Grande, Via Capodimonte. Tel: 081 749 9111; www.napolibeniculturali.it.
Open: Tue–Sat 10am–7pm, Sun 9am–2pm. Admission charge. Bus: 24, 110, R4.

Osservatorio astronomico

From below the ground to above the stars, the astronomical observatory was built in 1819 in order to take advantage of the clear views from the top of one of Naples' highest points. King Ferdinand I built this neoclassical structure soon after recapturing his lost throne. Check out the collection of equipment, both historic and modern, in one of Europe's first observatories of its kind. During the tour there are occasional opportunities to try out some of the tools of the trade, depending on the mood of your guide – so be sure to smile a lot and keep opinions to yourselves.
Salita Moiariello 16. Tel: 081 557 5111; www.na.astro.it.
Tours: Mon–Fri 9am–1.30pm. Bus: 24, 110, R4.

Parco di Capodimonte

The extensive parkland surrounding the highly recommended Museo di Capodimonte was originally intended for use as hunting grounds for Carlo III. For the best city views, go to the southern tip of the grounds past the Museo.
Porta Grande, Via Capodimonte.
Open: daily 8am–1hr before sunset. Bus: 24, 110, R4.

Parco di Capodimonte

Roman and ancient sites

If archaeologists had their way, the entire top metre of buildings, soil, dirt and residences that cover the city of Naples would be removed to give access to what lies beneath. A treasure trove of Greek and Roman remains lies under the city, almost, but not quite, within reach of scholars of the classical age.

Very little has been excavated, mainly due to the fact that it is almost impossible to dig up anywhere under the crowded and delicate streets that constitute the bulk of the Centro Storico. One wrong hole and an entire street could plummet into the ground below. One group that does its best to open up the mysteries of the earth is the Napoli Sotterranea. With its support a number of churches, including the Santa Chiara, Duomo, Santa Maria del Purgatorio ad Arco and San Lorenzo, have opened up sections of their grounds to provide a spectacular display of what lies below.

For the best ancient sites, you'll have to get yourself out of town. In addition to the world-renowned excavations at Pompeii and Herculaneum, there is evidence of Roman splendour dotted throughout the countryside – a testament to a time when the Campanian coast was a playground for the rich and famous of the day. The town of Baia and the Phlegraean Fields were particularly well loved by the upper classes for their famed curative waters. The geothermally heated spas and baths were favoured by a number of leaders, including Hadrian, Claudius, Nero and Caligula. Citizens looking for higher social standing and favours from the throne flocked to

SIBYLLINE SUPERSTITION

Campania has always produced its fair share of savvy wheelers and dealers, but never more so than the god Apollo's best-ever spokeswoman, the Sibyl of Cuma. Legend has it that in the 5th century BC, the Cuman Sibyl attempted to get her god more noticed by the Roman authorities. In a canny bit of Neapolitan mercantilism, the sibyl asked for an outrageous amount of money when she travelled to Rome to sell her nine books of Apollo's prophecies to the Roman King Tarquinius. Each time she was refused, the sibyl calmly threw three of the books into a fire. When she was left with three books, the superstitious king relented and the Cuman Sibyl got her original asking price. From that moment on, Apollo became an important god in the pantheon of Roman deities.

Parco Archaeologico di Cuma, Via Acropoli 1, Cuma. Tel: 081 854 3060. Open: daily 9am–1hr before sunset. Admission charge. Metro: Pozzuoli.

the area during the summer months, when the warm weather and cooling breezes attracted a who's who of Roman government. As such, the area established a reputation for gluttony, excess and ostentatious displays of wealth. It also became a favourite getaway for adulterous couples, and a place for sexual experimentation.

Emperor Tiberius loved the area so much that he temporarily moved his home to Capri, setting up house in the Villa Jovis on the eastern tip of the island. While little remains that suggests the level of splendour that once covered the Villa, a little bit of imagination should be enough to paint the frescoes and gilt work that once covered the region.

For a brief glimpse of the original 4th-century BC Greek city walls, hop over to the centre of Piazza Bellini. There isn't much to see, but the ruins give you an idea of just how far the city of Naples has spread since its days as the picturesque seaside port of Neapolis.

Bellissima Piazza Bellini

Pompeii, Herculaneum and Vesuvius

A visit to the towns that lie at the base of Vesuvius has been an integral part of a European's 'Grand Tour' education ever since the remains of the Roman town of Herculaneum were discovered in 1710. 'Yobbo' youths of yesteryear followed in the moneyed footsteps of millionaires from long ago by embarking on an extended visit to the region as part of their classical education – necessary for a respected position in the civil service or at royal court.

Today, a trip to Pompeii, Herculaneum and Vesuvius is less an educational stay and more a packed historical day trip away from the hustle and bustle of Naples. Considering the manner in which the treasures of the area were plundered by the Bourbons three centuries ago, excavations are surprisingly complete. While a knowledgeable archaeologist will shudder at the sight of primitive tunnelling techniques used in some of the oldest digs, the buildings and layout that remain give a surprisingly complete account of what life was probably like in the area almost 2,000 years ago.

Above the excavated sites and ancient homes lies one of Europe's most poverty-stricken communities. The stretch of Campanian coastline running from Portici to Stabia has some of the continent's highest unemployment rates and a level of urban blight and depression to match. A ride along the Circumvesuviana train line from Naples to your final destination is not a classic journey in any sense of the word. Graffiti-covered stations and crumbling apartment blocks testify to the area's long period of decline.

Rising above all the history and heartache is the symbol of Naples, towering Mount Vesuvius. While a constant plume of smoke no longer rises from this volcanic juggernaut, it is by no means dormant. Its last eruption in 1944 was extremely destructive, obliterating thousands of homes and heaping even greater problems on a population already distraught by the damage of World War II. Haphazard rebuilding has replaced everything that was lost in the post-war eruption; however, you can still see abandoned lava fields only a few kilometres away from densely populated communities.

With 1.5 million visitors arriving in Pompeii every year, the cost of maintenance and the demands for a tourist infrastructure are the greatest challenges of the area. Large-scale

The ruins of Pompeii

European Union developments are pumping money into the vicinity; however, there is a heavy push for increased privatisation in order to help cut costs in the cash-strapped Italian cultural heritage ministry. Plans are afoot to transform formerly 'lesser' excavations – such as those at Stabiae – into more popular destinations, with the aim of diverting the high tourist numbers away from Pompeii and into other communities in the region. Until an equivalent amount of investment money is pumped away from the usual two key archaeological sights (Herculaneum and Pompeii), this goal will remain just a pipe dream. Pompeii and Herculaneum remain the star UNESCO World Heritage Sites of the region and are well worth hours, if not days, of dedicated time to explore their hidden corners and walls of wonder.

POMPEII

On 24 August, AD 79, Vesuvius unleashed a sea of lava, ash and sulphurous gas onto the unsuspecting residents of the various towns and villages that dotted the base of the not-so-dormant volcano. Pompeii, the largest populated area other than Naples on the Campanian coastline, received the brunt of Vesuvius' hellish destruction. Luckily, modern-day archaeologists have two letters penned by Pliny the Younger, describing the violence of the eruption, with which they can develop modern-day conclusions as to the minute-by-minute effects of the eruption.

While Pompeii was a traditional holiday home for the rich and powerful of Rome, it had lost much of its popularity by the time Vesuvius decided to flatten it. Had the volcano decided to erupt a mere century earlier, half of Rome's elite and many of its most powerful leaders would have been killed. The rapid destruction of the town is perhaps best understood by looking at the plaster 'statues' cast from the reliefs left by bodies in the now-hardened volcanic mud. The finest examples are located on the top floor of the Museo Nazionale Archeologico in Naples.

As Pompeii is such a widely visited tourist destination and a UNESCO World Heritage Site, getting there is extremely easy – if sometimes a little crowded. Circumvesuviana runs frequent bus services from Via Pisanelli in Naples to Pompeii. Look for the stop located near Porto Immaeolafella. If

Pompeii and Vesuvius

The Great Palaestra

you have a rental car, the A3 will drop you right at the doorstep of the ancient town. Take the Pompeii exit from the A3 motorway and follow the stream of automobiles heading in the same direction. However, the traffic chaos of the region may make you think twice about considering either of the above two options. Road travel between Naples and Pompeii will take at least twice as long as you think it will, no matter what time of day you plan your departure. Trains are by far the easiest option. The Circumvesuviana railway (*tel: 081 772 2444; www.vesuviana.it*) runs frequent services from the Stazione Circumvesuviana, taking about 30–40 minutes. Be sure to get off at Pompeii Scavi-Villa dei Misteri station for direct access to ancient Pompeii. Fares depend on the distance travelled. Your best bet is to get a day pass covering Fascia 3 (Zone 3) between Naples and Pompeii. The cost is €4.60 and covers all your travel, including trips within the city of Naples, but can only be purchased after 10am.

If you plan on visiting a number of the five major archaeological sites (Boscoreale, Herculaneum, Oplontis, Pompeii and Stabiae), save yourself a lot of money by purchasing a cumulative ticket costing €20. Tickets are valid for three days and can be purchased at the ticket offices of any of the sites.

Scavi di Pompeii

Via Villa dei Misteri 2.
Tel: 081 857 5347; www.pompeiisites.org.
Open: daily Apr–Oct 8.30am–7.30pm; ticket office closes 6pm; Nov–Mar 8.30am–5pm; ticket office closes 3.30pm. Admission charge.

Walk: Pompeii in a day

This walk covers the best of Pompeii for those with a limited amount of time. Ideally, a visitor to the area would have days to explore its countless hidden corners of splendour, sleepy side streets and examples of ancient Roman life.

Count on spending at least 3 hours on this walk. It begins at the main ticket office close to Pompeii railway station. Note that some buildings may be closed for restoration. Check at the ticket office for details.

1 Porta Marina

This gateway to the city is one of seven original gates – and the most imposing – leading into the town. Porta Marina was the gateway closest to the sea, hence its name. It has two barrel arches and is surrounded by 3,200m (3,500 yd) of city walls.

Continue straight along Via Marina, past the Tempio di Venere. The Basilica is on your right.

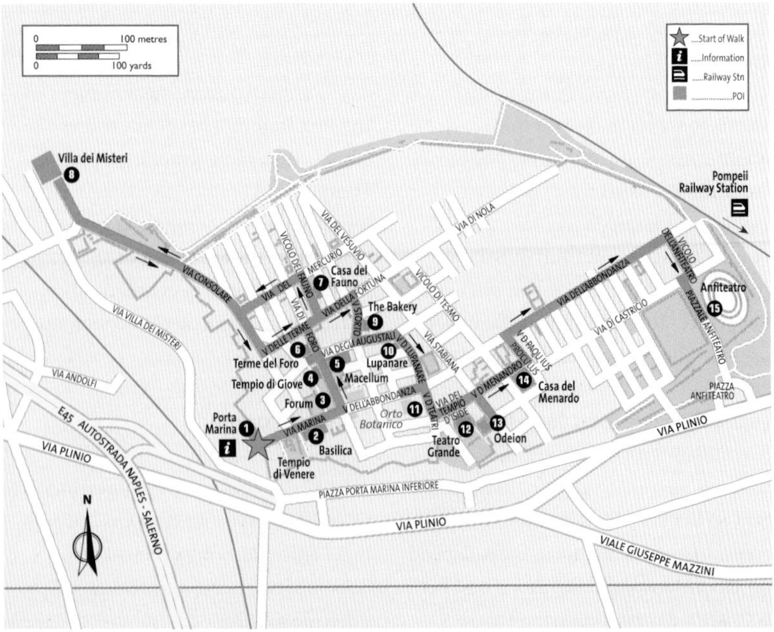

Basilica

2 Basilica

This rectangular building was built in the second half of the 2nd century BC. It has three naves, a sloping ceiling and columns and half columns. The court of law was situated at the back of the building and was reached via a wooden staircase.

Continue up Via Marina. The Forum is on your left.

3 Forum

The Forum was the town's main square of activity, surrounded on all sides by religious, political and business buildings. Its position at the intersection of two main roads, and the fact that this was a pedestrian zone, meant that the forum was at the heart of residents' daily life.

Continue up Via di Foro away from the Forum. The Tempio di Giove is on the left and the Macellum is slightly further along on the right.

4 Tempio di Giove

Pompeii's most important place of worship, this temple was dedicated to the god Jupiter – chief deity of the Roman religion. Already severely damaged in a previous earthquake, Vesuvius polished off the rest of the building, leaving little to behold today.

5 Macellum

This is ancient Pompeii's original meat and fish market. The 12 plinths in the centre of the courtyard once supported posts, which in turn supported a conical roof. The bases in front of the entrance portico would once have held commemorative statues to illustrious inhabitants.

When you approach the end of Via di Foro turn left. The Terme is immediately on the right.

6 Terme del Foro

The tiny baths at the top of the street were built after 80 BC. Though small, they are noteworthy for their original stucco decoration and well-preserved marble fountain. Bathtime was normally in the early afternoon.

With your back to Via di Foro take the first left into Vicolo del Fauno. The Casa del Fauno is on the right.

7 Casa del Fauno

The House of the Faun is one of the largest and most sophisticated in Pompeii. Named after the small bronze statue found in the middle of the marble *impluvium* (a low basin in the

This mural showing Venus rising from the sea can be seen at the Casa della Venere in Conchiglia, Pompeii

centre of a household), it is decorated in paintings and mosaics depicting the Battle of Issus in 330 BC between Alexander the Great and the Persian Emperor Darius III.

Continue up Vicolo del Fauno and turn left into Via del Mercurio, then right into Via Consolare. Go straight on for a long stretch.

8 Villa dei Misteri

The Villa of Mysteries has one of the most important decorative and fresco collections in the Roman world. Experts believe that the frescoes lining the *triclinium* (dining room) depict a woman's initiation into the cult of Dionysus, though others believe it is her initiation into marriage, hence the name of the villa.

Head back down Via Consolare before turning left into Via delle Terme, going straight on until it becomes Via della Fortuna. Turn right into Vicolo Storto. The Bakery is on your left.

9 The Bakery

This is actually one of 34 bakeries identified in the ruins of Pompeii so far. What makes this so special is the wood-burning oven, so beloved of pizzerias throughout modern Italy, and the surviving four millstones used to grind the wheat to produce flour.

Continue down Vicolo Storto and turn left into Via degli Augustali, then turn right into Vicolo del Lupanare.

10 Lupanare

One of the most infamous and titillating houses on the itinerary, the Lupanare was a popular brothel. The name is derived from the Latin for prostitute, *lupa*, and this one is la crème de la crème of Pompeii's many bordellos. There are stone beds in the little cell-like rooms, as well as a latrine. Frescoes on the walls depict the various positions punters may have used in these very rooms.

Continue down Vicolo del Lupanare and turn right onto Via dell'Abbondanza. On your left is the entrance to the Botanical Gardens.

11 Orto Botanico

A green haven in the midst of the dusty ruins, the Botanical Gardens have been restored with many herbs and plants grown that would have been found in Pompeii's heyday. Take time for a drink and a rest.

Exit where you entered, turn right and right again into Via dei Teatri. Turn left into Via del Tempio d'Iside and right into Via Stabiana. This is the entrance to the theatre complex.

12 Teatro Grande

This stunning theatre, built in the 2nd century BC, was dug out of the slope of the terrain, ideal for creating the tiers of seats. The theatre has a backdrop of the Sarno river plain and the heights of the Monti Lattari.

13 Odeion

The Odeion is the 'small theatre', probably used as a concert hall for musical performances and poetry readings. From inscriptions unearthed at the site, apparently the theatre had a permanent roof to provide excellent acoustics.

Return to the theatre complex entrance and go back up Via Stabiana. Take the first road on your right. Casa del Menardo is on your right.

14 Casa del Menardo

NB This house can only be visited by pre-booking.

The House of Menander was built in the 3rd century BC and was renovated and extended throughout the centuries. It possibly belonged to the Poppaei family, who were related to Nero's second wife. Much of the house remains in good condition, with a small temple, a marble *impluvium* and bathing area. To the left of the entrance, a room contains paintings depicting the Trojan War and in the so-called green hall there is a fresco depicting cherubs playing among grapevines. The house takes its name from the Greek playwright Menander as there are painted niches representing him.

From the house, turn right onto Vicolo del Menandro and left into Vicolo di Paquius Proculus. Turn right into Via dell'Abbondanza and go straight on until you reach Vicolo dell'Anfiteatro on your right.

15 Anfiteatro

Small by Roman standards, this amphitheatre could only hold around 20,000 spectators. Built in 80 BC, this elliptical structure was the site for the city's gladiatorial games. It is probably the best-preserved structure of its kind, complete with three sections of seats and a series of *vomitoria* (entrances) at the top.

HERCULANEUM

In many ways it could be argued that the remains and treasures of Herculaneum are even greater than those at Pompeii. Unfortunately, two millennia of population growth have built up over the ruins, leaving much of the city buried under a sea of high-rises and concrete.

Unlike Pompeii, death came painfully slowly to the residents of Herculaneum. Citizens thought they had escaped the worst of the destruction, until heavy rainfall hit Vesuvius, transforming the earth into a sea of mud, lava and ash that hurtled down the mountainsides directly on top of the city. This torrent covered the ancient ground level to a depth of over 20m (65ft), making eventual excavation extremely difficult, while ensuring that the remains were left in a remarkably good state of preservation.

Getting to Herculaneum is even easier than getting to Pompeii as it's situated under the city of Ercolano, approximately halfway between Naples' Stazione Circumvesuviana and Pompeii. Once again, driving is ill-advised, due to the traffic that plagues the roads of the Campanian coastline. If you must get behind the wheel of a car, follow the A3 motorway to Ercolano and follow the signs to Scavi di Ercolano. As per the standard rules of Neapolitan driving, finding a parking space will require nerves of steel. If you find somewhere to put your car, park it as soon as you can.

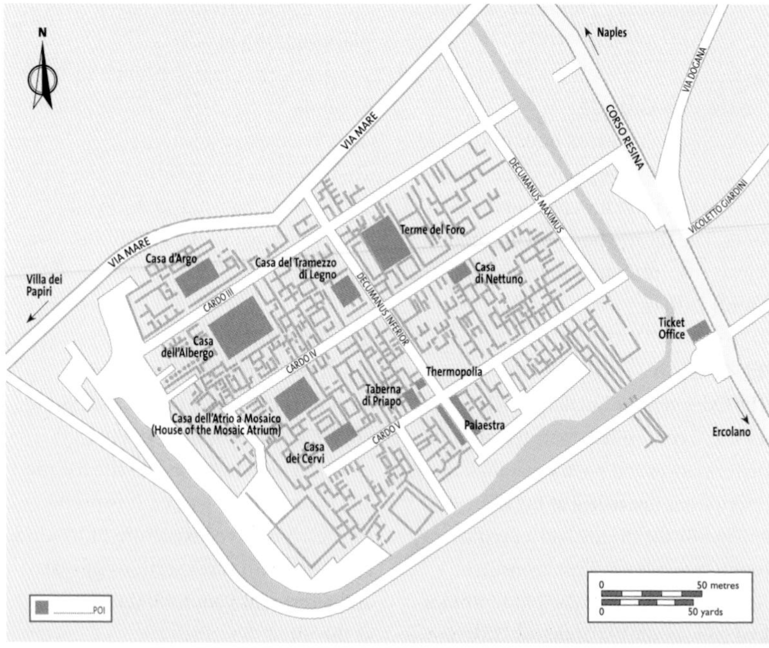

House of the Relief of Telephus

Buses are also available via ANM lines (*www.anm.it*), bus 157 from Piazza Municipio or 255 from Piazza Carlo III. Your best bet is the Circumvesuviana railway from Stazione Circumvesuviana on Corso Garibaldi. If you aren't going on to Pompeii, purchase a Fascia 2 (Zone 2) day pass for €3.60 and get off at Ercolano. This will be valid for your transport to and from the archaeological site and for travel within the city of Naples.

While there is a tourist office in Ercolano, it isn't one of the better ones. Staff at this office will give basic information about the area as well as maps to neighbouring Portici. English usage among staff members is limited.

Ercolano itself is best avoided. The town is one of the region's poorest, and architectural interest in the modern high-rises is extremely limited. The main street was at one time an extremely salubrious address for the wealthy of Naples. Considered the heart of the Miglio d'Oro (Golden Mile) of residential homes for court members of the Kingdom of the Two

Palaestra

Sicilies in the 19th century, Ercolano boasted a bevy of luxurious homes designed by the finest architects of the day. Following the declaration of the Kingdom of Italy in 1860, this stretch of land lost its importance and therefore its residents. Many of the palaces were abandoned for generations and left to ruin. Today, the avenue and its collection of villas have been left to rot, concealed as they are behind rusting gates and crumbling masonry. Many have been divided up into tiny flats, with little remaining of their original architectural interest.

Scavi di Ercolano (Herculaneum)

Corso Resina 6. Tel: 081 777 7008; www.culturacampania.rai.it. Open: daily Apr–Oct 8.30am–7.30pm; ticket office closes 6pm; Nov–Mar 8.30am–5pm; ticket office closes 3.30pm. Admission charge.

HERCULANEUM: A BRIEF HISTORY

Legend has it that the town of Herculaneum was founded by Hercules upon his return from Iberia. Records written by historian Sisenna describe the city as 'built on a small promontory by the sea and bounded by two rivers'. Herculaneum passed through the hands of the conquering Greek and Samnite empires before forming an allegiance with Rome at the end of the Samnite Wars in 290 BC.

Even though only a small section of the town has been excavated, what has been dug up reveals that Herculaneum was a centre of importance to the Roman Empire. Luxurious residences stood on the promontory and there is no evidence of wheel ruts on any of the paved streets to indicate frequent trade or passage of carts. As such, it is believed that Herculaneum was a wealthy residential location for the ultra-rich, chosen for its beauty, tranquillity and healthy environment.

THE BEST SITES

Casa dei Cervi

Named after its two marble groupings of deer being attacked by hunting dogs, the Casa dei Cervi (House of the Deer) is one of the most luxurious residences discovered in Herculaneum. Look for the grand dining room, decorated with frescoes and floored with one of the most elegant pavements in the Roman Empire. Almost all types of marble used during the 1st century AD can be found somewhere in the intricate flooring.

Casa del Tramezzo di Legno

Two atria in this house suggest that this building was originally divided into two residences and joined together sometime in the 1st century AD. A wooden partition (now carbonised) can be seen dividing the atrium to create a reception room where the master of the house would conduct his business.

Casa dell'Atrio a Mosaico (House of the Mosaic Atrium)

Named after its beautiful black-and-white chequerboard mosaic flooring in the atrium, this house is divided into three areas separated by two rows of pillars. In its day, the house enjoyed some of the best views in Herculaneum.

Palaestra

Known more for what it doesn't have than what it does, most of the Palaestra's grandest treasures have been removed and transported to the Museo Nazionale Archeologico for storage. Only partially excavated, the Palaestra has a frontage of 78m (255ft), making it one of the largest buildings in Herculaneum.

Terme del Foro

Herculaneum's public baths are notable for their stunning mosaics. Of particular note is the Mosaic of Triton in the women's baths.

Villa dei Papiri

Situated outside the main site, near the bookshop, this amazing building is now open to the public without the need to book in advance. Over 1,000 papyrus scrolls were found here, as well as 87 sculptures, which are now at the Museo Archeologico in Naples.

UNLOCKING HERCULANEUM

Wear and tear over the years has taken its toll on the ruins of Herculaneum. That fact, combined with the limited funds given to the site by the Italian state, means that only a few of the houses are open on any given day. Much of the town is permanently covered by nasty red fencing, thus ensuring that a number of your photos will be permanently scarred by manufactured reminders of the modern age. A list of open buildings is always displayed in the ticket office on the Corso Resina.

PORTICI

Europe's most densely populated town was devastated in the eruption of Vesuvius in 1631. Luckily a golden age of reconstruction and regal splendour wasn't too far behind. Following the dawn of the Bourbon age, King Charles III ordered a new palace to be built over the wasteland that covered the area. Court life brought the Neapolitan nobility to Portici and a new resort catering to the rich and favoured was born.

No longer the playground paradise it once was, concrete and construction plagues this town. For an idea of what Portici would have looked like, you should head directly to the palace and its grounds; however, you will have to use a lot of imagination.

Museo Ferroviario di Pietarsa

Europe's biggest and best railway museum is housed in the converted terminus building of Italy's first railway line. Inaugurated in 1839, the track stretched between Portici and Naples, with factories and workshops installed just over a year later. The museum currently occupies what were the original workshop buildings. All of the buildings have been authentically restored to accommodate the period locomotives on display.

Via Pietarsa, Portici. Tel: 081 472 003; www.ferroviedellostato.it. Open: Sun–Fri 8.30am–1.30pm.

Reggia di Portici and Orto Botanico

The palace that made Portici the heart of the Campanian court no longer sees much action. Three architects and hundreds of other specialists were integral to the splendour of the immense façade.

The grounds boast over 500 species of plant. The structure originally had two separate sections – the lower section faces the sea, while the upper section looks towards Vesuvius. The Reggia was essentially Naples' first archaeological museum, following the discovery of the ruins of Herculaneum, Pompeii and Stabiae. All of the pieces excavated during the early years were shipped directly to the palace for the pleasure of Charles, his son Ferdinand and the members of the royal court. Since 1873, the palace has been owned by Naples University.

Via Università 100. Tel: 081 775 4850; www.museiagraria.unina.it. Open: Reggia Sept–Jul Mon–Fri 8am–7pm. Gardens Mon–Sat 7am–1pm. Admission charge.

STABIAE

When the main coast road was completed, it bypassed the historic town of Castellammare di Stabia and sparked a 30-year decline. Once known for its shipyards and spas, the Castellammare is now banking on its proximity to the ancient ruins of Stabiae to ensure its survival. Ferry and hydrofoil services make it a convenient jumping-off point to the islands if you want to avoid the chaos of Naples' Molo Beverello. To get to the Castellammare di Stabia, take the Circumvesuviana train running between Naples and Sorrento. Travel time from Naples is about one hour.

Funivia and Monte Faito

The perfect summer getaway, Monte Faito is a pleasantly cool set of woodlands set on the higher grounds that overlook the town. Enjoy the numerous tree-lined walks and bask in the fresh, alpine air. Birdwatchers will love the ample opportunities to see robins, nuthatches and other native species that flock here during the summer months. The cable-car ride on the *funivia* is almost enough to warrant the trip alone. Before embarking on any hikes of the peak, make sure to pack enough water and food for the journey, since there are no dining facilities.
Stazione Circumvesuviana, Castellammare di Stabia.
Tel: 081 879 3097; www.vesuviana.it, www.profaito.org.
Open: daily Apr–mid-Jun, Sept, Oct 9.35am–4.25pm; mid-Jun–Jul 7.25am–7.15pm; Aug 9.35am–10.15pm.
Admission charge.

Scavi di Castellammare (Stabiae)

Of the digs along the base of Vesuvius, the excavation at Stabiae ranks as one of the most neglected. Work on Stabiae began at approximately the same time as the discoveries of Pompeii and Herculaneum were made; however, money and skilled workers were taken away from the area during the 18th century in favour of Pompeii. Excavations resumed in the 1950s, only to be set back yet again following the earthquakes in 1980. Visitors are limited to only two of the excavated villas, Arianna and San Marco. Most of the grandest artefacts, including frescoes and mosaics, were removed from the villas 200 years ago.

Décor and artwork in Villa San Marco are more impressive than in the walls of neighbouring Arianna; however, there are still great examples in each locale. Both villas cover large grounds, as their original owners continually added to the existing structures in order to show off their increasing wealth.
Via Passeggiata Archeologica.
Tel: 081 871 4541; www.pompeiisites.org.
Open: daily Apr–Oct 8.30am–7.30pm; Nov–Mar 8.30am–1 hr before sunset.

Villa San Marco

Hiking Vesuvius

While the lush green mountainsides of Vesuvius look calm, you shouldn't be fooled. This deceptively innocuous peak has been the cause of the death of thousands, the destruction of numerous homes, and has been the bane of more than just a few empires.

Vesuvius could erupt at any time, according to the experts at the Osservatorio Vesuviano, the institute that has monitored the volcano's activity since 1841. And even though locals have slowly reclaimed Vesuvius' slopes, you shouldn't follow in their footsteps: while 700,000 residents call the slopes of Vesuvius home, you can be pretty sure that the population figure will fall if and when Vesuvius decides to erupt again. When Vesuvius does decide to wake up, experts believe that ash and lava won't constitute the greatest risk. Rather, it will be a rapidly moving, super-heated cloud of gases that will cause the most destruction – much like the one in AD 79.

No visible reminders of the volcano's hazards have remained since

Vesuvius looms over the ruins of Pompeii

the last time Vesuvius decided to blow her top in 1944. There is no plume of smoke, flowing lava or floating ash; even the vegetation has grown back, with native plants returning to the rich volcanic soil located at the top of the cone.

A walk up the peak is a popular pastime and well worth considering even if you aren't a regular hiker. Declared a UNESCO Biosphere Reserve, the volcano is a protected plot of land attracting 200,000 visitors each year. Hiking is permitted right up to the rim of the cone, allowing visitors to peek down into the depths of the crater 200m (656ft) below. Best in May and early June, Vesuvius should be tackled in the early morning on calm, clear days. Windy days are not advised, as conditions on the exposed rim during these periods can be critical. The standard 30-minute route runs between the 'Quota 1,000' car park and the rim along a well-maintained, curving path. The car park is located at the end of the road on the mountain's western side. An interesting museum and observatory, chronicling eruptions of times past and the history of volcanic study, is located on the way to the car park along the western road. The Bourbon-period building in which it is located has survived at least seven eruptions and countless generations of smoke, fire and lava.

Colourful volcanic rock

Bus and car are the best ways of getting to the area. **Trasporti Vesuviani** (*Tel: 081 963 4420*) runs regular services up Vesuvius from Piazza Anfiteatro in Pompeii, passing by the Ercolano station on the Circumvesuviana train line. From this route you can both visit the Observatory and get dropped off at the car park to begin your hike. One-way transport from Pompeii costs €3; from Ercolano the cost is €1.70. By car, drive along the A3 motorway to Ercolano and follow the signs to Parco Nazionale del Vesuvio.

Cratere del Vesuvio

Tel: 081 771 0939. Open: daily 9am–2hrs before sunset. Admission charge. Note that trips to the crater are suspended during bad weather.

Museo dell'Osservatorio Vesuviano

Tel: 081 610 8483; www.ov.ingv.it. Open: Sat, Sun 10am–2pm. Free admission.

Capri

'Capri combines, in a granite basket, all the most colourful and fragrant species of Mediterranean flora. It is a land naturally dedicated to the repose of the mind and the delight of the senses, an Insula Beatorum, *a floating Garden of Eden.' So wrote Alberto Savinio: popular since Roman times, so much has been written about this craggy corner of Campania.*

During the Romantic period, writers, artists and poets flocked to the island to experience the 'lost sensuality' portrayed by the topography and Capri's inhabitants. Capri's modern-day popularity was cemented in the 19th century with the discovery of the Grotta Azzurra (Blue Grotto), but its sun-drenched shores had been beckoning tourists and travellers for at least two millennia before that time.

From remotely Roman to courtly capital

Capri captivated a number of Roman emperors, but none more so than Tiberius, who spent the last ten years of his life ruling the empire from his Villa Jovis. Tiberius ruled by using a courier service and was unseen by citizens of the capital, fuelling rumours of his scandalous lifestyle – rumours that weren't entirely unfounded. Following his death, the island fell into a long period of decline. From the Middle Ages onwards, the rocky shores fell into the hands of a number of rulers and were the scene of more than a few skirmishes, most notably between the English and the French during the Napoleonic Wars.

Invasion of the tourist

Capri was far from ready to deal with the mass tourist influx that coincided with its popularity in the romantic literature of the 19th century. As writers such as Henry James and Goethe spread the word about Capri's trappings and charms, tourists travelled to the sleepy island to find out what all the fuss was about – and they haven't left since. The invention of the hydrofoil was the best (or worst, depending on how you see it) boost for local tourism, as the months between June and September see up to 50,000 visitors descend upon the landmass every day. Every year the mayor of Capri announces plans to limit daily visitor levels to a more manageable level; and every year absolutely nothing is done. No matter how many people decide to hit Capri, the rocky topography and small-scale agriculture translates into a number of quiet nooks and crannies available for exploration.

Luxurious lifestyles

In order to maintain its exclusive reputation, the hotels of Capri charge notoriously outrageous prices: a simple coffee on the *piazzetta* can cost an arm and a leg in high season. Traditionally, those who want to 'see and be seen' stick to the properties around Capri, while fans of solitude and a more down-to-earth atmosphere head over to the agricultural trappings of Anacapri. But the big draw of the island continues to be the fabled Blue Grotto, 'discovered' by a Polish poet called Kopisch, but known by the residents and fishermen of the island for years. A typical visit to the Blue Grotto takes about two hours out of your sun-bathing and shopping time, with numerous boats departing from the Marina Grande throughout the day.

Arco Naturale

TRAVELLING TO CAPRI

There are a number of ways to get to the island of Capri. The most common method is via the numerous ferries and hydrofoils that ply the waves between the major ports of Campania and Capri's Marina Grande. From Naples' main commuter port, the Molo Beverello, services run throughout the day. There is also a scheduled service from Mergellina and the western end of the bay.

Should Naples prove incompatible with your itinerary, you can reach the 'playground of the rich' from Sorrento, Ischia and the Amalfi Coast ports of Salerno, Amalfi and Positano. For daily updated timetables, check the Naples newspaper *Il Mattino*. Once on the island, the **Capri Tourist Board** provides a wealth of information, including a listing of all return sea schedules. Before you arrive in Naples, check out the Capri Tourist Board website (*www.capritourism.com*) for seasonal crossing times and prices. While services from Naples run all year, transport between the Amalfi Coast, Ischia and Capri only runs in high season, from April to October.

Schedules and services

From the Amalfi Coast: LMS (*Tel: Amalfi 089 873 301/Salerno 089 234 892/089 227 979*) runs hydrofoils and ferries between Amalfi, Positano, Salerno and Capri. **Consorzio Linee Marittime** (*Tel: 089 873 301*)

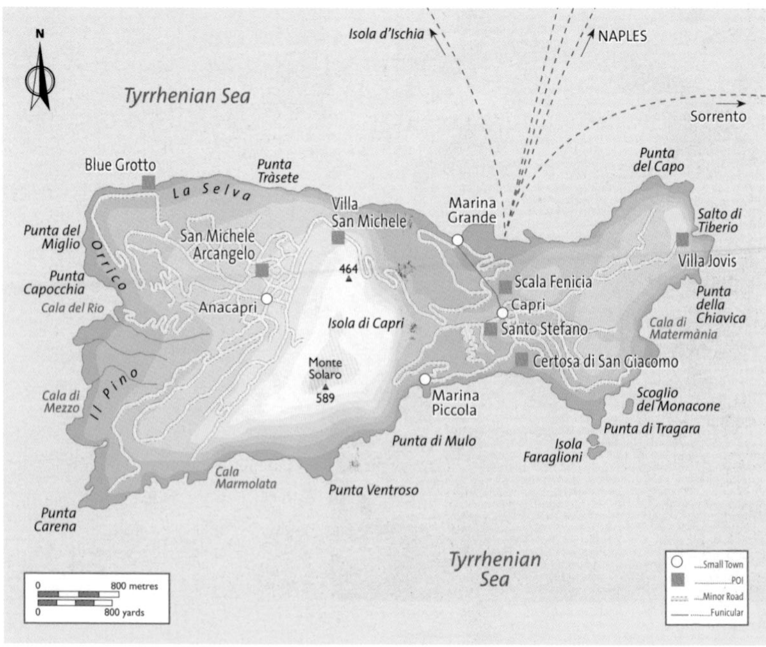

Punta Carena

Enjoy boating around gorgeous Capri

runs hydrofoils from Positano only. Journeys take approximately 30 minutes.

From Ischia: Alilauro (*Tel: 081 497 2238*) runs hydrofoils daily from Ischia Porto. Hydrofoils take 40 minutes to make the crossing.

From Naples: Caremar (*Tel: 081 017 1998*), **Alilauro** (*Tel: 081 497 2238*) and **Medmar** (*Tel: 081 333 4411*) are the main companies that run between the Molo Beverello and Capri. In summer, hydrofoils run hourly between the Molo's central quay and the Marina Grande. By hydrofoil, the crossing time is approximately 40 minutes.

If you prefer using a ferry, **Caremar** is the company to choose. Six daily ferries run all year round from Beverello – three of which are high-speed *traghetti veloci* (50 minutes); the others take 1 hour 20 minutes. Ferries are both cheaper and the only option in rough weather. Last boats from Naples usually leave at 8.30pm in winter and 9.30pm in summer.

From Sorrento: Caremar (*Tel: 081 017 1998*) and **LMP Alilauro** (*Tel: 081 497 2238*) make the 20-minute crossing from Sorrento's Marina Piccola to Capri. In summer, hydrofoils leave on an hourly basis.

By helicopter: The transport option of choice for visiting dignitaries, Hollywood celebrities and Middle Eastern royalty is also the most expensive. The cost of a one-way flight accommodating up to four people from Capodichino airport to the Anacapri heliport is €1,500. *Contact Cab Air, tel: 081 789 9022; www.cabair.it*

By water taxi: If you're in a rush or travelling out of season, water taxis are available from most ports on the Campanian coast. **Taxi del Mare** (*Tel: 081 877 3600; www.taxidelmare.it*) is the most common line, offering a fleet of ten-seat speedboats at a rate of €32 per nautical mile. A typical run from Sorrento to Capri will set you back about €275 one way.

Getting around

Capri town is closed to all forms of motorised transport beyond the bus terminus on Via Roma. One exception to this rule (and a great help to people with various mobility problems) is the electric trolleys that transport luggage between the marina and the numerous hotels.

Five-star properties usually offer porters at quayside, should you require them. If you have a large amount of luggage, you should take advantage of this service, as the cliffs of Capri are quite steep and difficult to traverse, especially during the tourist-choked peak season when waiting times to use the funicular railway can get long. Look for the name of your hotel on the cap of the porters as you disembark from your ferry or hydrofoil. Anacapri hotels offer minibuses to bring you and your luggage directly to the door. Otherwise, the funicular, buses and taxis are all available at the end of the quay. If you are planning to do a lot of touring around the island, take advantage of the Unico Capri public transport ticket, available from the funicular ticket office. Tickets come in three options – single trip, 60 minutes

Capri town

and day-pass – and can be used throughout the entire network.

Circle-island boat tours: Circuit tours of the island can be booked at the Marina Grande from a number of tour operators. Tours sometimes include the Blue Grotto, depending upon weather conditions. Prices start at €15 per person.

By bus: There are six bus routes that can take you to most corners of Capri. The three main services that run most frequently are Marina Grande–Capri (*6am–midnight*), Marina Grande–Anacapri (*6am–7pm*) and Capri–Anacapri (*6am–2am*). The other three routes of Capri–Marina Piccola, Anacapri–Grotta Azzurra (Blue Grotto) and Anacapri–Punta Carena run less frequently, especially in the off season. For information call **ATC** (*Tel: 081 837 0420*), except for the Blue Grotto and Punta Carena lines, which are operated by **Staiano** (*Tel: 081 837 2422*).

By funicular railway: From the main Marina Grande station, funiculars

Shopping in Capri

View from Monte Solaro

tackle the climb to Capri town every 15 minutes (*Apr–Jun 6.30am–10.10pm; Jul–Sept 6.30am–11pm; Oct–Mar 6.30am–9pm*). The funicular is operated by **SIPPIC** (*Tel: 081 837 0420*).

By scooter: If you have the guts to try it out, a scooter can be the fastest and most economical way of getting around Capri. Rent a scooter at **Rent an Electric Scooter** (*Via Roma 68. Tel: 081 837 5863*). Scooter rentals cost €20 per hour, including a helmet. A driving licence is not required. As the scooters are electric, they have a limited range of 50km (31 miles) before they need recharging at the base: but don't worry about getting stranded, as this is a lot of distance on this tiny landmass.

By taxi: Capri's taxi fleet is one of the best-looking in the business. Open-topped vehicles can take you anywhere on the island – albeit at a price. The tiny streets make overtaking almost impossible, so if you get stuck behind a slow-moving vehicle, be prepared for a long journey and a high fare. Typical rates are €15 from the port to Capri town or Anacapri, and €100 for a circle-island tour.

THE GROTTA AZZURRA (BLUE GROTTO)

Capri legend has it that Polish poet August Kopisch and Swiss artist Ernst Fries discovered the Blue Grotto in 1826 after swimming here accompanied by a local hotel owner and fisherman. Truth be told, islanders had known about Capri's most famous sight for centuries – a landing stage and small, rough-hewn nymphaeum dating back to the period of the Roman Empire can be found at the back of the Grotto – and often played practical jokes on visitors exploring the area. Local writer Raffaele la Capria backs this claim, suggesting that the discovery of the grotto was merely a prank played on the two artists after being lured by tales of 'a cave inhabited by the devil… and by strange marine creatures'.

Today, a ride to the Blue Grotto requires more than just an eager guide. The most common method of reaching the cave is by motor launch from the Marina Grande. The three-stage journey involves a quick motorboat ride to the Grotto, a transfer to a four-seater rowboat and a lightning-flash row under the low-lying cave entrance into the mystical blue beyond. The whole trip costs about €15. You can save yourself €1.50 by taking the bus from the Marina Grande, changing at Anacapri for travel to the car park above the Grotto. While you may not save much money, it makes for a delightful way to familiarise yourself with the lie of the island. Tours of the Blue Grotto, including travel time to and from the famed cave, take about an hour and a half. For maximum time

Boats at the Grotto Azzurra

Inside the famous cave

inside the cave, avoid the peak season and/or plan your visit late in the day or during the lunch hour when demand to get inside the Grotto is at its lowest.

The Grotto owes its exalted position in Capri's list of tourism draws primarily to the wealth of literature and writing dedicated to its enchanted qualities. One anonymous 19th-century English traveller outlined the best way of seeing the Grotto's delights by stating that 'a visit requires a cloudless day, a resplendent sea in a placid bay, the dazzling skies of Italy should abate, and the very breezes be calm and still'. The anonymous traveller got it quite right when describing ideal conditions, as the mystical blue appearance of the Grotto is caused by the refraction of light. Calm seas translate into greater refraction and a more intense blue colour on the walls of the Grotto and vault.

Theoretically, you can still enjoy a visit to the Grotto by swimming through the entrance after paying the standard €4 entrance fee. Kopisch and Fries may have enjoyed this method of examining the Grotto's trappings back in 1826, but today's intrepid few are advised not to attempt this foolhardy way of entering the cave. Strong currents and the possibility that the boatmen who transport tourists in their sturdy rowboats may strike you on the head with one of their oars are the two biggest reasons to discourage you from donning your bathing costume.

High winds and rough seas close the Grotto on a regular basis, especially between November and March. Check postings at the Marina Grande for further details.

Open: daily 9am–1hr before sunset.

Hedonistic Capri

Capri may be the playground of today's nouveau riche, but the level of excess seen in modern-day hotels, yachts and restaurants pales in comparison to the hedonism of yesteryear. The island's salacious history dates back to AD 27, when Emperor Tiberius visited Capri during a tour of southern Italy. Tiberius was so enchanted by Capri's people and geography that he moved himself and his entire court to the island to live out the last ten years of his life here.

During his time on Capri, Tiberius developed a number of strange and highly erotic tastes, often demanding large groups of young male and female servants 'perform' in front of him. When that failed to appease his voyeuristic nature, he wandered through the grounds of his lush villa complex – the Villa Jovis – to enjoy the numerous erotic statues, Egyptian love manuals and descriptive paintings.

After earthly pleasures, torture was second on Tiberius' list of favourite things to do. Torture rooms, prisons and execution chambers existed in all of the villas owned by Tiberius on the island. The 330m (1,083ft) Salto di Tiberio precipice, found at the end of a long loggia in the northern end of

The view from Villa Jovis

The home of Curzio Malaparte

the Villa Jovis grounds, is thought to have been where enemies of the state were thrown to their death into the rock-strewn waters below.

Pink Capri

While loved by the effete American author Truman Capote, Capri is no longer the pink mecca it once was. The mid-20th-century decades saw the straight literary set move in, banishing the gay community to other, more accepting locales. In their place arrived Maxim Gorky, Lenin and a collection of Russian émigrés, author Graham Greene and Curzio Malaparte – an Italian Ernest Hemingway, famous for his exploits in the 1940s and 1950s.

THE KRUPP AFFAIR

Greeks and Sapphics weren't the only ones to bring scandal to the shores of Capri. Friedrich Alfred Krupp (1854–1902), a German steel heir and industrialist, was so intoxicated by the island that he built a roadway from the steps of his private villa down to the Mediterranean. Hewn from the rocky slopes of the island, the Via Krupp winds its way down from the heights of Capri to the Marina Piccola. The breathtaking, yet narrow, road remains one of Capri's most pleasant walks – unfortunately, Krupp's personal fate wasn't as 'happily ever after'. In 1902, Krupp committed suicide after accusations were raised that he had been taking part in orgies in one of the island's grottoes. It is still unknown to this day as to whether Krupp was involved in the scandal or if the accusations were part of a political plot to smear his name.

CAPRI TOWN

Capri town is both the height of luxury and an example of how awful the tourism industry can get. Packed with five-star celebrities and no-star package-trippers, the place still manages to draw in a who's who eager to figure out what's what.

Certosa di San Giacomo

This ancient monastery at the eastern end of the Via Matteotti was built by a monastic order that was established in 1371 by Count Giacomo Arcucci, the powerful secretary to Queen Joan I. Islanders have never held strong affections for the residents of the monastery, often coming into conflict with them over the island's hunting and grazing rights.

During the plague of 1656, tensions reached a high point as the monks locked their doors to the outside world, refusing to tend to Capri's sick and dying in the hope of saving their own lives. In response, locals threw the bodies of the plague-infested dead over the monastery walls.

Casa Rosa

Marina Grande

Almost everyone's first port of call upon reaching Capri is the bustling Marina Grande. During the high season, the marina is a hellish mass of humanity. Get out as fast as you can – and that might take a while, judging by the usual length of queues to get on the funicular up to the centre of town. If you are looking to tour around the island, then you're in the right place. From the Marina Grande, you can purchase boat tours, hire a taxi, catch a bus to Anacapri or buy public transit passes from the main ticket office.

Piazzetta

Look to the left as you emerge from the funicular station at the far end of the Via Roma. Here you will find Capri's 'see and be seen' heart, the Piazzetta. Packed with cafés and pedestrians, the Piazzetta is the archetypal Mediterranean town square. Four rival bars, indistinguishable from each other except by their different-coloured chairs, take over the square, providing the best opportunities for gossip and

The view from Scala Fenicia

catching up on the latest in couture fashion trends. While the coffees are expensive, the social theatre on display will more than make up for the exorbitant cost.

Capri's parish church, **Santo Stefano** (*Open: daily 8am–8pm*), is located on the south side of the Piazzetta. There isn't much of note about the Baroque architecture, other than the fact that it was built on the same site as an earlier church.

Via Vittorio Emanuele III

Capri's main street runs south from the Piazzetta past dozens of high-fashion boutiques and *limoncello* souvenir outlets. Some of the big names to look out for include Cavalli, Dolce & Gabbana, Zegna and Gucci. Most of the clothing boutiques are stocked with the dregs of the collections – suitable only if your Vuitton luggage was accidentally lost in the first-class check-in lounge.

Villa Jovis

An easy walk from Capri town is the Roman home of Emperor Tiberius, the Villa Jovis. From the Piazzetta, the Via Botteghe leads past the Chapel of San Michele. Follow the path past the church until the houses thin out and the hike gets steep. The actual villa isn't as impressive as it most certainly once was; however, you can still see the Salto di Tiberio – a precipice from which Tiberius executed criminals – and remnants of the huge cisterns that guaranteed the self-sufficiency of the complex.

A corner of the Villa San Michele gardens

ANACAPRI

Anacapri retains a distinct small-town feel in comparison to its more upmarket neighbour, thanks to the fact that it was separated from the rest of the island by an impervious wall of cliffs until a connecting road was finally built in 1877. Less village and more a collection of small-scale farmers and residents, Anacapri is the laid-back holiday alternative on the island. Mentioning the word *dolce* here will bring you a delicious pastry, and not a luscious designer gown from the catwalks of Milan.

Rural residents and *caprese* rivals

The *anacaprese* are fiercely independent individuals. For years, locals preferred to travel to the Neapolitan ports in search of work rather than owe their salaries to the enemy *caprese* a few kilometres down the island. Until the construction of the inter-island road, the only means of getting to the remote cliff-side community was via the Scala Fenicia, a steep set of stairs that leads up from the Marina Grande. Travellers from Anacapri to Naples were forced to go through the port, deep in enemy territory, whenever they needed to visit the mainland.

Fame and fortune

Anacapri owes its illustrious reputation to the writings of the 19th-century Swedish doctor Axel Munthe. While researching his book *The Story of San Michele*, he encountered the local postmistress on the street. She informed him that she had 'once been down to Capri – but it hadn't impressed her much'. Munthe later incorporated this episode into his work and translated his tales of life in the southern climes into over 30 different languages. The book is littered with representations of the quirky rural folk that inhabited this tiny corner of the island back in the 19th century. Northern Europeans in turn flocked to the tiny village to discover its rural charms.

San Michele Arcangelo

The town's major church is a piece of Baroque splendour, boasting a

wonderful majolica mosaic floor based around the theme of earthly Paradise. Built in 1761, the floor is a particular favourite with children, due to the numerous representations of exotic animals in the brightly coloured tiles.
Piazza San Nicola. Tel: 081 837 2396. Open: daily Jan 10am–2pm; Feb, Mar, Nov, Dec 9.30am–4.30pm; Apr–Oct 9am–7pm. Admission charge.

Villa San Michele

Making his fortune as the hottest society doctor in Paris, Axel Munthe moved to Anacapri 15 years after first setting foot in the village in 1874. Using the funds he had built up in his prime medical practice, he built the Villa San Michele on the grounds of one of Tiberius' original 12 Capri villas. The architecture mixes Renaissance and Romanesque influences with a large number of statues.

The actual building isn't worth more than a cursory exploration, but the views are definitely worth the trip. The villa and gardens are kept meticulously clean, thanks to a Swedish foundation that keeps the Munthe flame alive. Try to time your visit with the Friday-evening classical music concerts held in the gardens during the summer.
Viale Axel Munthe 34. Tel: 081 837 1401; www.sanmichele.org. Open: daily Mar 9.30am–4.30pm; Apr, Oct 9am–5pm; May–Sept 9am–6pm; Nov–Feb 9am–3.30pm. Admission charge.

Villa San Michele

Ischia

Lying at the western end of the Bay of Naples, Ischia, along with the neighbouring islands of Procida and Vivara, forms the Phlegraean archipelago. The volcanoes that formed the bays, sheer cliffs and caves are now extinct, yet the geothermal springs remain, drawing thousands of tourists each year to the healing waters.

While the island of Capri has always had an intoxicating effect on those who visit its shores, Ischia has historically been more of a slow-burning destination. When the Greeks arrived in the 8th century BC, they quickly departed in favour of the mainland camp at Cuma. The island's seismic activity and population of indigenous residents didn't suit the newcomers at all, even though Ischia was ideally suited as a strategic position on the Mediterranean trade routes.

During the Roman era, the island finally found fame through its geothermally heated waters. It retains this reputation today through the huge number of spas and hydrotherapy centres that continue to populate the area.

The last eruptions on the island occurred in 1302. Fearing another Pompeii, residents fled to the mainland in Baia, only returning to the Ischian shores four years later when they gathered on the rock of the Castello Aragonese – a castle built to protect Ischia from the constant invasions of foreign powers and pirates.

Ischia fell into the hands of various conquering foes throughout the centuries, eventually succumbing to the British allies of King Ferdinand following a decade of French rule.

W H AUDEN

Writer W H Auden spent almost all of his time between the years of 1948 and 1957 on Ischia. Renowned as a haven for gay pleasure seekers, Ischia's rocky shores welcomed Auden and he fell in love with the sleepy fishing village of Forio, calling it 'one of the loveliest spots on earth'. His love affair with the island fell apart after he hired a notoriously handsome local boy named Giocondo to look after his house. In 1956, Giocondo tried to cash a cheque Auden had given him. Giocondo claimed it was for 'services rendered', causing fury among island residents and the parish priest. The feud and disgust caused Auden to flee the island for Austria, never to return. 'I don't like sunshine,' he commented. 'I would like Mediterranean life in a northern climate.'

The British took years to oust their hated enemies from the island, bringing intense devastation. Evidence of their bombardment can still be seen on the castle's walls.

The north coast of the island remains the most populated coast, due to the easy access to the sea and picture-perfect views of the Phlegraean Fields on the mainland. The best day to celebrate its climate, thermal waters and stunning beaches is 26 July – the date of the procession to honour Ischia's patron saint, Sant'Anna.

TRAVELLING TO ISCHIA

Ischia is as easy to get to as Capri – the only difference being in the companies that choose to ply the waters between the mainland and Ischia Porto and/or Casamicciola. Departures to and from Capri, Sorrento and Procida are also available, albeit far less frequently.

During low season inter-island departures may be delayed or terminated, so it is best to check in advance if you are planning a complicated itinerary. From the main commuter port of Naples, the Molo Beverello, departures run throughout the day. There is also a scheduled service from Pozzuoli and the western end of the bay. For daily updated timetables, check the Naples newspaper *Il Mattino*.

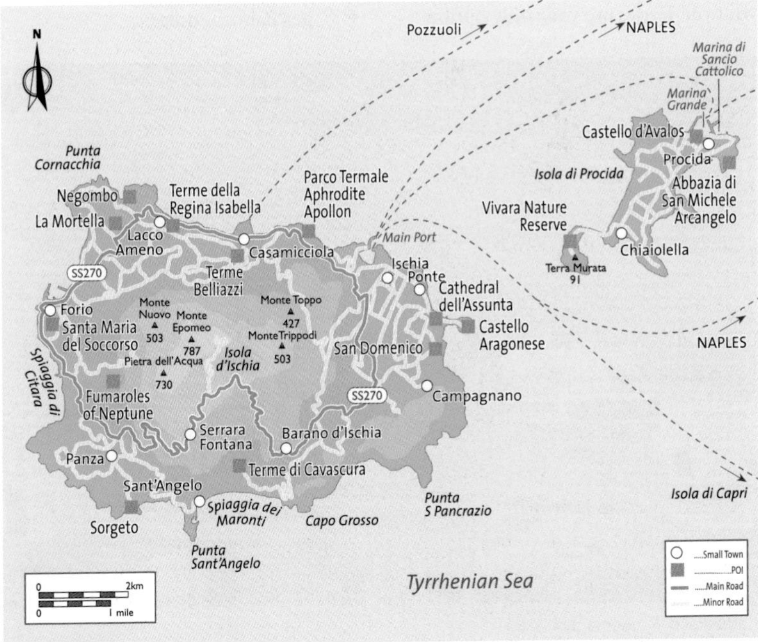

Schedules and services

From Naples, Pozzuoli, Capri, Sorrento and Procida: Caremar (*Tel: Call centre 892 123/from abroad: 0039 0226 302 803; www.caremar.it*), **Alilauro** (*Tel: 081 497 2238; www.alilauro.it*) and **Traghetti Pozzuoli** (*Tel: 081 333 4411*) are the main companies that run hydrofoil and car ferry services between the mainland, the Bay of Naples archipelago and the Ischian ports of Porto and Casamicciola. Hydrofoils run hourly between the Molo's central quay and Ischia Porto. By hydrofoil, the crossing time is approximately 45 minutes. The cost of a crossing is approximately €15, depending on the company.

If you are planning on transporting your car, ferries are your only option, and they take approximately 1hr 35min to complete the journey. Ferries are also cheaper, and they are the only option in rough weather. Tickets start at €9 if you are travelling without a car. Last boats from Naples usually leave at 8.30pm in winter and 9.30pm in summer. A charge applies if you make an advance booking – well worth it during high-season weekends. Note that credit cards are only accepted when booking online.

By water taxi: If you're in a rush or travelling out of season and are pressed for time, water taxis are available from most ports on the Campanian coast. **Taxi del Mare** (*Tel: 081 877 3600; www.taxidelmare.it*) offers a fleet of ten-seater speedboats at a rate of €32 per nautical mile.

Cathedral dell'Assunta, Ischia

Ferry to Ischia

Circle-island boat tours: If you would like to see Ischia from a different perspective, consider a boat trip with **Capitan Morgan** (*Tel: 081 985 080; www.capitanmorgan.it*). Tickets cost €15 for a circle-Ischia tour, or €30 for a day-trip to Capri.

Getting around by bus: Ischia's public transport services are run by **Eavbus** (*Tel: 081 542 9614; www.eavbus.it*). The two main routes you are likely to encounter are the *circolare sinistra*, which circles the island in an anticlockwise direction from Ischia Porto, and the *circolare destra*, which does the same route clockwise. Stops include Casamicciola, Lacco Ameno, Forio, Serrara Fontana and Barano.

Services run every 30 minutes (every 15 during the rush hour) and tend to get packed during the high season.

BE YOUR OWN CAPTAIN

If a luxury yacht isn't within your budget or you're short of that million or two to sail your way around the Med, don't fret! Procida may be a tiny island, but it's big on choice when it comes to chartering your own boat. Its new yacht marina – the biggest in Campania – has drawn a number of savvy entrepreneurs to its snazzy docks, making it an excellent place to arrange an Italian sailing holiday. Rental periods can cover anything from a day-trip to a month-long cruise. Choose your own adventure with the following rental outfits:

Ippocampo
Lato Ponente (west side), Marina Chiaiolella. Tel: 081 658 7667; www.ippocampo.biz.
Open: Mar–mid-Oct daily 9am–7pm. No credit cards. Rates from €75 per day.

Sailitalia Procida
Via Roma 10, Marina Grande. Tel: 081 896 9962/800 220 008; www.sailitalia.com.
Open: Mon–Sat 9.30am–1.30pm, 3.30–7.30pm. No credit cards. Rates from €1,200 per week.

Other services include routes from Ischia Porto to Sant'Angelo (every 15 minutes), Giardini Poseidon to Citara (every 30 minutes) and Spiaggia dei Maronti via Testaccio (every 20 minutes).

Minibus services run within Ischia Porto, Ponte and Forio. Tickets are required before boarding and can be purchased at the terminus in Ischia Porto, at *tabacchi* stores and in news-stands. At time of writing, tickets cost €1.50 (single trip), €6 (24hr), €15 (weekly pass) and €22 (two-week pass).

North Ischia

Always the busiest part of the island, the north coast of Ischia boasts a number of sights and villages to explore, suitable both for day-trippers and those on an extended stay. Once two separate towns (Villa dei Bagni and Borgo Celsi), the main strip of hotels and shops has been combined into one administrative centre known as Ischia Porto and Ponte. This area incorporates the entire stretch of coast between the ferry port and the Castello Aragonese.

Castello Aragonese

Originally fortified by the Greeks in the 5th century BC, this rocky outcrop has been used as a stronghold by just about every group, empire or army intent on conquering the area. Romans, Goths and Arabs have all had their hands on the Castello – but never for very long.

The Castello found fame in the 16th century when it became home to the court of Vittoria Colonna, the wife of Ischia's feudal lord, Ferrante d'Avalos. Vittoria had a strong – albeit platonic – relationship with Michelangelo, who ensured her memory would live on in

Castello Aragonese

Forio is Ischia's leading wine-production area

his work. 'Nature, that never made so fair a face, remained ashamed, and tears were in all eyes,' he wrote after watching Vittoria pass away in 1574.

With the Saracens a constant threat to Ischia's fragile population, the Castello became a refuge of sorts, calling itself home to 2,000 families. Even after the Saracen menace disappeared in the 18th century, locals insisted on staying within its formidable walls.

It took 100 years for the families to move out, leaving behind about 13 churches and a few nuns to run the place. The British managed to damage the Castello more than any other invading force during their bombardment of the island in 1809. Determined to rid Ischia of its French 'rulers', they attacked the Castello: you can still see the scars of their aggressive actions pockmarked on the walls. Following the success of the British military plan, the fortress was transformed into a prison to accommodate French prisoners of war. *Tel: 081 992 834; www.castelloaragonese.it. Open: daily 9am–7.30pm. Admission charge.*

The main port

Until 1854, Ischia's main port was an inland lake formed by an extinct volcanic crater. The waters, due to the geothermal activity of the area, were particularly smelly. King Ferdinand II was so repulsed by the odour that he ordered that an opening should be constructed linking the waters to the sea. And so a port was born.

Hot-tubbing Ischia

If you're looking for the ultimate in relaxation, then you've come to the right place. Ischia has been famous for its thermal baths since the days of the Roman Empire, when visitors would flock to the bubbling pools that dot the island for healing and curative rest. Thanks to the geothermal power of the Phlegraean Fields, Ischia (then called Aenaria) was the area's most popular holiday resort for the rich and unwell. Its mysteriously soothing powers remain popular today – even if hedonists come just for the pleasure of a soak in a naturally warm hot tub.

True connoisseurs have a favourite rest stop, selecting their top-bath list according to mineral content and success rates in curing particular ailments. But, with 103 hot springs available on the island, you'll have plenty of options to choose from.

The cove at Negombo

Unfortunately for people on a tight budget, most of the hot springs have been commandeered by hotels and resorts that allow access only to paying guests, but there are still a few open to all if you look for them. The following are some of the better possibilities:

Negombo

Baia di San Montano, Lacco Ameno. Tel: 081 986 152; www.negombo.it. Open: mid-Apr–mid-Oct daily 8.30am–7pm. Admission charge.

A public spa open to day visitors. Entrance allows access to a stunning garden filled with hundreds of exotic plants, the San Montano beach and the obligatory thermal spa facilities.

Parco Termale Aphrodite Apollon

Via Petrelle, Sant'Angelo. Tel: 081 999 219; www.hotelmiramare.it. Open: Apr–Oct daily 8.30am–6pm. Admission charge.

A popular option for fans of letting it all hang out, the Parco Termale offers a nude bathing area, massages and medical treatment. Free boat-taxis from Sant'Angelo are included in the admission fee. Saunas, a gymnasium and 12 pools are available with the purchase of a day pass.

Negombo mineral spa

Terme Belliazzi

Piazza Bagni 134, Casamicciola. Tel: 081 994 580; www.termebelliazzi.it. Open: Apr–Oct Mon–Sat 7am–noon, 5–7pm. Admission charge.

If you want to experience what drew Roman tourists, then visit the baths of the Terme Belliazzi. Built over the site of the original ancient Roman pools, the architecture is firmly neoclassical in tone, looking much like a temple in honour of the body. Massages, whirlpools and mud treatments are all on offer to those who want a little extra.

Terme della Regina Isabella

Piazza San Restituta, Lacco Ameno. Tel: 081 994 322; www.reginaisabella.com. Open: Apr–Oct Mon–Sat 8am–12.15pm, 5–7.30pm, Sun 8am–12.15pm. Admission charge.

A rare example of a hotel that allows entrance to day visitors who purchase a pass. All of the usual treatments and baths are on offer, albeit in a slightly grander style than you might normally get in some of the other public-access properties. The price of a day pass is slightly higher than in other locations, but in this instance you most certainly get what you pay for.

Terme di Cavascura

Via Cavascura, Spiaggia dei Maronti, Serrara Fontana. Tel: 081 905 564; www.lapalmatropical.it. Open: mid-Apr–Oct daily 8.30am–1.30pm, 2.30–6pm. Admission charge.

Ischia's most naturally beautiful spa, the Terme di Cavascura is hewn out of rugged cliffs located at the end of one of Ischia's most stunning hikes. Designed for the truly knowledgeable spa-goer, treatments on offer include massages, facials and thermal baths in divine locations – including a natural cave.

Ischia's main street is the **Via Roma**. Pedestrianised to accommodate the hustle and bustle of activity during the high season, it is lined with numerous exclusive shops and hotels. North of the Via Roma is where you will find the town's main beach. Take any of the lanes leading off the street to find your way there.

If you need a break from the beating sun, follow the traffic to the junction with Via d'Avalos. A gate just off the main strip leads to a lush (and slightly unkempt) garden in the grounds of the **Villa Nenzi Bozzi**, which is filled with shady trees. *The gardens are open daily 7am–8pm.*

Campagnano

Just before the SS270 enters Ischia town, a quick turn-off leads to Campagnano. There isn't all that much to warrant a visit, except for the church of **San Domenico**. Known primarily for its 19th-century majolica decorations on the façade, the church is a delightful location for a photo opportunity, thanks to its views of Ischia Porto and the Castello Aragonese on the cliffs below.

Forio and the west

Forio is the largest town on Ischia, with a year-round population of 20,000 people. Twelve ancient watchtowers line

Forio, Ischia

the coast near the Ischian 'metropolis', originally built to help guard the city's population against the constant Saracen attacks that plagued the area. The best example that remains standing today is **Il Torrione**, dating from around 1480.

While there are 17 churches to choose from in town, most have been highly remodelled and no longer feature original artwork. The one exception is the church of **Santa Maria del Soccorso**. Originally a 14th-century Augustinian convent, its white outline in the centre of a large viewing platform makes it one of the most romantic churches on the island.

The narrow road leading to Monte Epomeo gives some idea of the importance of wine-making in the region – and the length of time residents have lived in the area building the industry up to its current peak. The meandering roadway is lined with vines covering a number of rock-cut troglodyte dwellings, and evidence of habitation goes as far back as the Stone Age. Today, Forio is Ischia's leading wine-producing centre.

Before you leave town, be sure not to miss the **Fumaroles of Neptune** and the thermal complex in the **Bay of Citara**. Botanists should also add the gardens of **La Mortella** to their list of 'must-sees'. The lush, green space calls itself home to more than 3,000 types of plant, most of which are extremely rare.

La Mortella: Via F Calise 39, Forio. Tel: 081 986 220; www.lamortella.org.

La Mortella

Open: Garden Apr–Oct Tue, Thur, Sat, Sun 9am–7pm. Concerts Apr–Jun, Sept, Oct Sat, Sun 5pm; arrive 30min early, to ensure seating. Admission charge.

Monte Epomeo and the southwest

Monte Epomeo is Ischia's highest peak at 787m (2,582ft). Lying to the east of Forio, the mountain can be traversed by taking Via Monterone or Via Bocca to the paths that lead through the Falanga forest to the summit. Note, however, that the paths are poorly marked and easy to miss, so keep your eyes peeled.

If you find the town-centre beaches a little too crowded for comfort, the southwest is where you will find the **Spiaggia di Citara**. Most of this sandy

Boats at Sant'Angelo

stretch is owned and operated by the Giardini Poseidon, but you can still find pockets of free access here and there. Consider biting the bullet and buying a day pass for true pleasure.

For free hot-spa action, head on down to the hidden secret of **Sorgeto**. A particular favourite among locals, Sorgeto can be reached from the tiny village of **Panza**: directions are tricky, so be sure to ask a local for advice if you get lost. Signs exist in Panza directing you to Sorgeto; however, they look like they haven't been changed since Roman times! Follow a series of

HIDDEN CORNERS

For something a little out of the ordinary, try exploring the deserted coves that line the southern cliffs of Ischia. Sant'Angelo makes for a perfect departure point if you want to enter nooks and caves that feel like they've never before been seen by human eyes (even if your boat driver has already brought 20 couples and a tour group to the same cove earlier that day). Rent a boat-taxi from the main docks and tell the driver to take you to the stretch of land between the two ends of the Spiaggia dei Maronti. Be sure to negotiate your rate before you step into the boat, making sure that the quoted cost is for a round-trip adventure.

sharp curves in the road and a long flight of stairs and you will eventually find yourself at a rocky cove. A spring gushes through the rocks and into the sea at a constant temperature of 32°C (90°F). This is a perfect locale for combining a dip in the sea with a spot of soothing relaxation in the heated pools.

The south

The sights of the southern coast of Ischia are dictated by the route of the SS270 road. Towns along this stunning route include Serrara Fontana and Barano d'Ischia. None of the villages features anything of architectural note, but the views overlooking the sea are incredible. If you are trying to reach the summit of Monte Epomeo from the town of Fontana, follow the road marked *strada militare* and *vietato l'ingresso* (no entry) up to the top. The route is perfectly legal until you reach the bar-restaurant just before the military zone. Drive your car to this point and walk the short distance to the top. The walk should take approximately 40 minutes if you take the path to the left of the metal bar that crosses the road. From the summit there is a magnificent 360° view over Ischia.

Spiaggia dei Maronti

Sant'Angelo
Ischia's most picturesque village, Sant'Angelo, is a multicoloured (ex)-fishing hamlet perched above the extraordinarily blue waters of the Mediterranean. While the town draws many international tourists – largely due to its proximity to the 2km (1¼ mile)-long beach of the **Maronti** – Sant'Angelo is largely a playground for locals. However, the beach, while still a draw, is no longer what it once was. The sea and numerous storms have eaten away much of the sand. The eastern end is reserved mostly for family-friendly fun, while geothermal activity on the western flank reserves the steamy pools for fans of heated splendour. This is where you will find the Parco Termale (*see p116*).

PROCIDA

Covering less than 4 sq km (1½ sq miles), Procida is the most densely inhabited island in the Med. The sea and its treasures provide the bulk of the island's employment opportunities – the island has produced fishermen and merchant sailors for generations – with luxury yachts pouring into the new Marina Grande on a daily basis.

First populated by the Greeks, small fishing villages prone to attack were built on the island's shores. Locals quickly realised that life on the high grounds was the only possible defence against invaders and proceeded to pack up their homes in favour of hillside residences and the island developed a prosperous shipbuilding and fishing industry. Procida continued to experience periodic raids and pirating until the Bourbon age when the royal family purchased the Castello d'Avalos and turned the area into a hunting reserve. Locals were banned from owning cats, which might destroy the stock of pheasants, and were subjected to heavy fines. Needless to say, the Bourbons weren't exactly well loved by the local populace. By this time, however, the bulk of Procida's residences were owned by prosperous vacationing mainlanders who built summer homes on the island's rocky shores.

Today, the Good Friday procession is Procida's claim to fame. The Processione dei Misteri involves a life-size wooden sculpture of Christ on the Cross, carried by local fishermen to the Marina Grande under a black veil. Other wooden sculptures follow the main statue, carried by men dressed in white cloaks with turquoise capes and children in medieval costume.

You won't need any form of transport other than your own two feet on Procida – the island is that small. A complete circuit around the island takes approximately four hours, if you're fit.

A brief word of warning to anyone contemplating a trip during peak season: while Procida is the least visited of all the islands in the region, it is also the smallest. Consequently, the shores are practically heaving with humanity, exploding from a year-round population of 11,000 to almost 20,000 in August. Despite this, there are still undiscovered pockets to explore, even during the height of summer. Enjoy watching the daily catch come in, as you sit at one of the cafés that line the Marina Grande, or savour a stroll through one of the inland lemon groves and you'll be sure to fall in love with Procida's numerous charms.

The architecture of the island is one of the most distinctive in the region. Small, multicoloured homes rest against the tufa rock, nestled next to each other tighter than sardines in a tin. Unique to Procida are the vaulted buildings built to house boats during the winter season and enlarged over a number of generations to incorporate arches, frames, terraces, windows and other forms of exterior decoration. Examples of this quaint architecture can be seen on your arrival in Procida's **Marina di Sancio Cattolico**.

Abbazia di San Michele Arcangelo

The main port of Procida, in existence almost since the first day the Greeks

Procida's Marina Grande

Distinctive Procida architecture

explored the area back in the 5th century BC, owes its current look to a mini-population boom in the 17th and 18th centuries. The most famous sight on the island remains the Abbey of San Michele.

Dating back to 1026, the abbey has been rebuilt a number of times since the original structure was erected, and it boasts a painting by Luca Giordano of the archangel Michael. The interior is worth exploring for its large manuscript library, museum, Nativity scene and labyrinthine catacombs leading to a secret chapel.

Via Terra Murata 89.
Tel: 081 896 7612;
www.abbaziasanmichele.it.
Open: Apr–Oct Mon–Sat 10am–12.45pm, 3–6pm; Nov–Mar daily 9.45am–12.45pm. Church free. Admission charge for museum, library and catacombs.

Castello d'Avalos

You may not be able to enter its foreboding walls today, but up until 1986 you wouldn't have wanted to. Castello d'Avalos was Italy's answer to Alcatraz – an island prison where only the most dangerous or important offenders were sent. The massive structure will be the first building you see if you arrive at Procida's main port by ferry. As yet, there are no plans to open up the building as a tourist attraction.

HIKING THE ISLANDS

A hike through the islands of Capri, Ischia and Procida is both a popular way of getting around the tiny landmasses and a great way to enjoy the archipelago's stunning views. **Terra Murata**, Procida's highest point, is a mere 91m (300ft) above sea level, so even the most out of shape should find a brief hike relatively easy.

Capri and Ischia make for more challenging treks. The path connecting **Monte Solaro** (589m/1,932ft) to Anacapri is extremely popular and may even feel something like a busy high street on Christmas Eve if you decide to tackle it during the high season. Ischia's famed trek is the route up the extinct volcano, **Mount Epomeo** (787m/2,582ft). Climbs to the summit usually start before dawn to ensure a view of the sunrise when you reach the top.

Chiaiolella

Procida's second most popular ferry port is also its most beautiful. The marina is virtually untouched since the day the ancient structure was built, nestled in a secluded bay brimming with gardens, greenery and the lemon trees for which the region is famous. The **Vivara Nature Reserve** takes advantage of the very fertile soil of the area, displaying numerous examples of Mediterranean flora, fauna and bird life. You can reach the reserve from Chiaiolella's marina by using a bridge that links Procida to the small island on which the park is situated.

Riserva Naturale di Vivara: No phone.
Open: Mon–Sat 8.30am–noon;
last entry 10am.

The Amalfi Coast and Sorrento

Just when you thought that nothing could beat the hustle and bustle of Naples, the sun-kissed splendour of Capri or the ancient mysteries of Pompeii – along comes the truly magnificent Amalfi Coast. The twists and turns of state road 163 as it leads you through this paradise suspended between the earth, sea and sky may be perilous to navigate, but most of life's best things come at a price.

Until the 19th century, the towns, caves and cliffs of the Amalfi Coast were almost impossible to reach by land. Travellers looking to discover their personal Eden had to do so by hiring pack mules to take them over treacherous mountain passes. Poets, artists and writers of the Romantic era

Sorrento

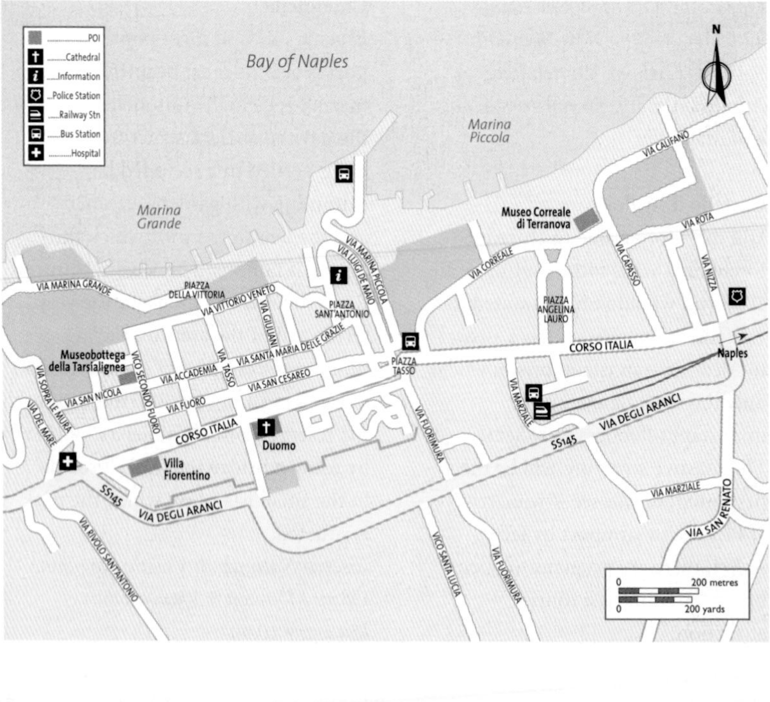

were drawn to the area for precisely this reason, and the hordes soon followed. Up until this time, life on the Amalfi Coast was filled with hardships. Pirate raids, flooding, landslides, the battering sea and isolation attacked residents on an almost daily basis. A brief period in the spotlight during the Byzantine Empire shone brightly, yet remained extinguished for centuries until its fame came from a new and highly unlikely source – northern European tourists.

Today, the Amalfi Coast is pummelled with a different sort of daily attacker – the exhaust and gridlock formed when thousands of holidaymakers descend on the area every weekend from April through to October. If you decide to visit during this time, then you will spend most of your day stuck behind the wheel of your car. During these long periods of inactivity, a bottle of water and constant air-conditioning are musts.

Stretching from Punta della Campanella to Salerno, the Amalfi Coast can be approached from Sorrento via Sant'Agata sui Due Golfi (between the Bay of Naples and the Gulf of Salerno), via the Colli di Chiunzi or from the south via Salerno.

The Amalfi Coast

Statue of St Andrew, Amalfi

Whichever route you do decide to choose, you should be warned that the roads here are not for the faint-hearted. If you suffer from vertigo or a fear of sharp turns, then you might want to consider using one of the numerous tour buses that ply the route on a daily basis.

Three of the main centres along the route boast impressive tourism credentials. Visitors are drawn to Amalfi with its glorious past as a marine republic, the pastel-coloured, steep-sided fishing town of Positano, and Ravello, chosen by Wagner as the setting for his opera *Parsifal*. While it may be important to check off the list, you should by no means limit your explorations to the 'big three'. The Amalfi Coast is made to be explored, preferably at a leisurely pace. A car or coach may be necessary to discover the area's beautiful trappings, but it's the moments when you get out from behind the wheel that will truly inspire the heart.

Getting there:

From Naples airport

To Sorrento: Six coaches run in each direction every day between Naples airport and Sorrento with additional stops at Vico Equense, Piano, Meta and Sant'Agnello. The bus service is operated by **Autolinee Curreri Service** (*Tel: 081 801 5420*). One-way tickets cost €6 and are available on the bus.

To Positano: Take the coach service to Sorrento and change for **SITA** (*Tel: 081 752 7337; www.sitabus.it*) local bus services.

To Amalfi: Take the coach to Sorrento and change for SITA local bus services.

By boat

To Sorrento: Linee Marittime Gescab (*Tel: 081 704 1911; www.gescab.it*) and **Alilauro** (*Tel: 081 497 2238*) run year-round hydrofoil services between Naples' Molo Beverello and Sorrento. Linee Marittime Partenope services take 45 minutes and cost €9, while Alilauro is quicker at 20 minutes, costing €11.

To Positano: Depending on the time of year, there are one to four hydrofoils shipping passengers between the ports of Salerno, Capri, Amalfi and Positano every day. The most frequent service operates along the Amalfi–Positano route – unhelpful if you are trying to get to the coast from outside the peninsula. From June to September there is a non-stop service directly to Naples' Mergellina dock, run by **Gescab** (*Tel: 089 873 301*). It is also possible to take ferry services to Positano, connecting at Capri.

To Amalfi: Regular boat services operate from Salerno and are the cheapest and quickest alternative. **TraVelMar** (*Tel: 089 872 950; www.travelmar.it*) run ferries during the summer season from the Molo Manfredi dock in Salerno.

By bus

To Sorrento: SITA is the local bus service that operates all routes out of Sorrento across the Amalfi Coast. Services on Sundays and public holidays are extremely infrequent, often stopping completely by 7pm. Ticket prices vary according to distance travelled, with no ticket more expensive than €3.20. Services run hourly between 6.35am and 8.05pm along the main Sorrento–Positano–Amalfi route.

To Positano: One bus, run by SITA, departs Naples every day from Monday to Saturday, returning in the early evening. At all other times, take the Circumvesuviana train to Meta and change for the SITA-run Sorrento–Positano–Amalfi bus.

To Amalfi: Frequent services run between Amalfi and Salerno via Positano, Agerola or Vietri. From Naples, take the Circumvesuviana train and change at Meta for the Sorrento–Amalfi bus. Times and information can be found through SITA. Sunday services are extremely infrequent and unpredictable: avoid them if at all possible.

By car

To Sorrento: Take the SS18 coast road or the A3 motorway to Castellamare di Stabia. At the end of the motorway, follow the SS145 southeast around the peninsula. Avoid driving if at all possible. Sundays and the summer season can choke these roads with time-consuming traffic.

To Positano: Follow the directions to Castellamare di Stabia and turn onto the SS145. Turn onto the SS163 at Meta, 4km (2½ miles) east of Sorrento.

To Amalfi: Leave the A3 motorway at the Angri exit and follow the signs to the Valico di Chiunzi pass and Ravello.

By train

To Sorrento: Sorrento is the terminus of the Circumvesuviana railway (*Tel: 800 053 939*), which runs along the Bay of Naples coast from Naples. Services operate every 30 minutes in each direction. The last train leaves Sorrento at 11.26pm. A Naples–Sorrento ticket costs €3.30 and is valid for 3 hours.

To Positano and Amalfi: There is no Amalfi Coast train line. Travellers are advised to use other methods of transportation.

Sorrento

Purists sometimes argue that Sorrento isn't the real Amalfi Coast – it's too easy to get to, too packaged and too convenient for those who love the coast's more challenging trappings – but if it's geological splendour and a steep, cliff-hugging village you're after, then you've come to the right place (*see p126 for map of the town*).

The central location, good infrastructure and strong transport links make Sorrento a great place from which to explore the Amalfi Coast. And if Naples' chaos and traffic are getting to you, then the laid-back lifestyle of the town will make for a delightful change of pace.

Inhabited since prehistoric times, the area around Sorrento has been coveted for centuries. The Greeks adored it so much that Homer sent his hero Odysseus (or Ulysses in Latin) to endure the temptations of the peninsula's siren songs in the *Odyssey*.

After the Romans moved in, they transformed Sorrento from an important Greek trading post to a holiday home-away-from-home for the empire's elite. Luxury villas sprouted up all along Sorrento's coast – a trend that remains to this day along the more picturesque and secluded roads of the area.

Sorrento maintained independence of a sort throughout the turbulent years following the fall of the Roman Empire, eventually succumbing to the Lombards and the power of neighbouring Naples in the 12th century. Unshackling Sorrento from Neapolitan influence continues to be the number one wish of all Sorrentines to this day – a wish that will ultimately never be granted.

Duomo

The original cathedral of Sorrento was rebuilt during the 15th century in the Gothic style. Fine examples of local *intarsio* (wooden inlay) work decorate the choir stalls. Of particular note is the bishop's throne dating from 1573 and constructed from a collection of marble fragments.

Corso Italia. Tel: 081 878 2248. Open: daily 7.45am–noon, 4.30–8.30pm. Free admission.

Museobottega della Tarsialignea

Situated in a restored 18th-century palazzo, this museum holds some of Sorrento's best examples of locally produced *intarsio* (wooden inlay) furniture. Prized by collectors, Grand Tourists and nobility alike from the mid-18th century onwards, the intricate furniture displays local craftsmanship and artistry at its finest. Old paintings and photographs of Sorrento provide additional context. The gift shop is a must-see, riddled with modern-day interpretations of marquetry furniture. International shipping is available.

Via San Nicola 28. Tel: 081 877 1942; www.alessandrofiorentinocollection.it.

The Marina Grande, Sorrento

Open: Mon–Sat 10am–1pm, 3–6.30pm. Admission charge.

Museo Correale di Terranova

A haphazard collection of local art and artefacts left to the town by a pair of brothers in the 1920s. The archaeological section boasts the best exhibits, including a collection of Greek and Roman marbles, Greek classical sculptures covered in inscriptions in Doric dialect, the famed Sorrento Base (1st century BC), decorated with bas-reliefs depicting the religious policy of Augustus, Attic and Campanian vases and lapidary inscriptions. There are also minor works of 17th- and 18th-century artists and paintings by the Neapolitan school.
Via Correale 50. Tel: 081 878 1846. Open: Wed–Mon 9am–2pm. Admission charge.

Villa Fiorentino

A 19th-century villa operated by the local council. The public gardens are small, yet enjoyable on a hot summer day. The actual villa is only open on special occasions, for local art exhibitions or lectures on local history.
Corso Italia 53. Tel: 081 878 2284. Open: daily 9am–1pm, 3–10pm. Admission charge for exhibitions and events.

Positano by night

Positano

'Positano bites deep', according to US author John Steinbeck. 'It is a dream place that isn't quite real when you are there and becomes beckoningly real after you have gone.' Steinbeck wrote these words for *Harper's Bazaar* in 1953 after visiting this pastel-toned, steep-sided town during a tour of the area. For residents during the 18th and 19th centuries, however, everyday life in Positano was all too real. Life here was – and still is – vertical and exposed to the conditions. Vulnerable to pirate raids and lacking any industrial base, three-quarters of the population emigrated to the United States in the mid-19th century.

The peak of respectability

What makes for a bad lifestyle makes for a great tourist destination, as evidenced by the sheer number of tourists who visit this 'cliff with houses on it' every year. In the 1950s, Positano was a closely guarded secret, held dear by the Italian artists and writers who patronised its establishments. By 1960, the hotels, international tourists and rising starlets moved in, making it almost as popular as Capri as a place to see and be seen. If Capri was Bardot then Positano was more Garbo – famous but not wanting to make too big a statement about it. Its heyday is reflected in the modernist hotel architecture and numerous 1960s-style postcards on offer at souvenir stores throughout the village.

Foul fashions

If you've heard that Positano is a fashionable centre to make clothing purchases, then think again. While there are a number of boutiques to choose from, most of the proprietors opened their businesses during the peak of 1960s' resort-wear chic – and have yet to leave that tacky fashion era. It may be good for a last-minute purchase of a new swimming costume, but you'd be advised to leave the multi-coloured Hawaiian dresses alone.

Navigating the town

The buildings of Positano cling precariously to the hill, climbing it in steps with the oldest structures lying in the upper section, faded to a pale pink and decorated with Baroque stuccoes. **Via Pasites**, the pedestrianised street that runs vertically through the town, is the main street you will come to know and love if a visit to the sea is in your plans. Houses seem to defy the gods in their positioning.

Cooling down

Don't worry about the baking sun; there are plenty of options available if a dip in the water is to your liking. To visit inaccessible inlets or the islands of **Li Galli**, boats are available to rent or charter at the docks. If that proves to be out of your wallet's reach, there are beaches within walking distance at **Ciumicello**, **Arienzo** and **Fornillo**. In the case of Fornillo, a direct path from the marina will lead you to the sandy stretch with its two looming watchtowers. For something a little more secluded, try the grottoes of **La Porta** – home to a number of Palaeolithic and Mesolithic ruins. In all cases, be sure to bring a bottle of water and a towel. Facilities can be limited at some locations and the sun can get extremely hot. The entire region is far from wheelchair-accessible, so be sure that you are prepared for a strenuous day of walking.

Amalfi

Once a powerful maritime republic, the town of Amalfi seems to cling to both the rockface on which it nestles and its 11th-century heyday when the town led Italian commerce, rivalling Venice and Genoa in port traffic and trade. Amalfi's republic took up the entire Sorrento Peninsula and much, much more. Amalfitan sailors were respected across the continent, often hired to battle on behalf of not only the republic but also neighbouring allies.

While little remains from this brief golden age, a few things still hark back to the days when the town had a bustling population of over 60,000.

THE ANCIENT MARITIME REPUBLICS REGATTA

Every year, Italy's ancient maritime republics of Venice, Pisa, Genoa and Amalfi take it in turn to organise a regatta. Each town has a designated colour – blue in the case of Amalfi – and compete against each other for honour and glory. The events are preceded by a procession in period costume, bringing back memories of each city's past triumphs. The regatta is always held on the first Sunday in June. Hotels along the coast get fully booked up during this period and advance reservations are a necessity.

Duomo di Sant'Andrea

Amalfi's main cathedral was founded in the 9th century and rebuilt many times since. While the façade and atrium date back to the late 19th century, the bronze doors that feature in the centre hark back to the year 1000 when they were cast in Constantinople. The rest of the structure is a complete mishmash of styles, including an Italian Romanesque campanile (1276) and a divine **Chiostro del Paradiso** (paradise cloister) built for the Bishop Augustariccio in 1266 as a cemetery for the town's more fêted citizens.

From the cloister, a door leads into the **Cappella del Crocefisso**, the only part of the church to have survived relatively intact from the 12th century. Inside the chapel, glass cases hold the Duomo's treasures, including a 15th-century marble bas-relief and a bejewelled mitre made for the Anjou court of Naples in 1297.

Piazza del Duomo. Tel: 089 871 059; www.diocesiamalficava.it.
Open: daily Mar, Oct 9.30am–5.15pm; Apr–Jun 9am–7pm; Jul–Sept 9am–9pm; Nov–Feb 10am–1pm, 2.30–4.30pm. Admission charge for Cappella del Crocefisso.

Duomo di Sant'Andrea, Amalfi

Museo delle Carta

The **Valle dei Mulini**, with Amalfi at its heart, was the site of some of Europe's first paper-making factories. Watermills once dotted the landscape as they powered the factories that made the continent's earliest aids to record-keeping and storytelling. One of the original worksites, the **Palazzo Pagliara**, has been transformed into a museum, illustrating the history and techniques of the trade. Go downstairs to find original vats and machinery – some of which date back to the Middle Ages.

High-quality paper is still produced in the area by the **Cartiera Amatruda**, one of the oldest papermills, and can be purchased at boutiques and shops throughout the town.

Palazzo Pagliara, Via delle Cartiere 24. Tel: 089 830 4561; www.museodellacarta.it. Open: Apr–Jun, Oct daily 10am–6pm; Jul–Sept daily 10am–8pm; Nov–Mar Tue–Sun 10am–3pm. Admission charge includes tour in English.

The real Duchess of Malfi

The playwright John Webster was an extremely disturbed individual – at least, he was if you can judge him from his seminal work, *The Duchess of Malfi*. Filled with images of incest, murder, psychotic episodes, torture and a lot of blood, the play has been the plague of generations of confused students since it was written in 1613.

Set in Amalfi, the play was merely the third reincarnation of a tale that has been around since the 16th century. Originally a story written by popular Italian author Matteo Bandello in a collection of his shorter works, it was borrowed by writer William Painter for his work *The Palace of Pleasure*, and plagiarised in turn by Webster.

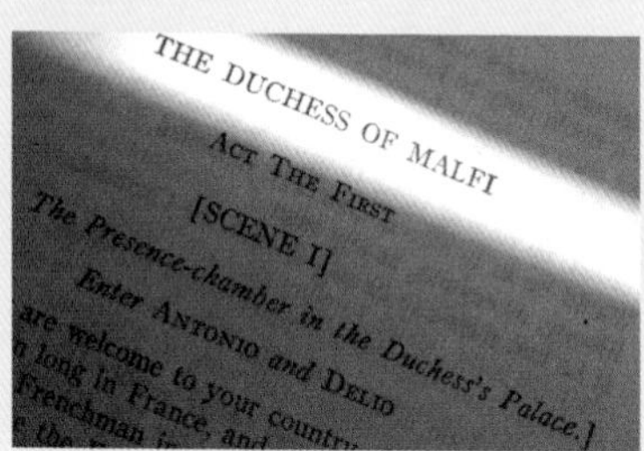

An extract from *The Duchess of Malfi*

Who is she?

All fingers point to Giovanna d'Aragona (Joan of Aragon) as the unfortunate duchess in question. Member of the ruling family of Naples, Giovanna was married off to Alfonso Piccolomini, the son and heir of the Duke of Amalfi, when she was just 12. Eight years later, Alfonso died of gout and Giovanna was left a widow, pregnant with her second child.

Determined to keep some independence and romance in her life, Giovanna started a passionate affair with her steward, Antonio Bologna. Romantic liaisons with commoners were unheard of during this time and Giovanna needed to keep her lips sealed – especially from her powerful brothers Carlo, the Marquis of Gerace in Calabria, and Lodovico, a cardinal.

Till death us do part

The couple managed to marry in secret and somehow kept the birth of two of their children away from palace spies in the pay of the brothers – until disaster finally struck. When Giovanna's clan found out about the forbidden love, Antonio fled with the two children to Ancona. Giovanna, pregnant again, followed a few months later and announced her intentions to renounce her rank and live humbly. The brothers thought otherwise and banished Antonio.

The plot thickens

It is at this point that Webster's story and the actual history of the duchess diverge. In Webster's masterpiece, the duchess is quickly set upon by palace spies and strangled. History, however, proves to be less tidy. Antonio and the duchess managed to live on the run throughout Italy for a number of years, until they were finally separated by a promise of safe conduct for them and their eldest son. Giovanna returned to Amalfi and effectively disappeared from all known records. Antonio survived until 1513, when he was stabbed to death by four hired assassins in a Milanese street.

Sets and locations

To see some of the more authentic duchess-related locations, check out **Torre dello Ziro**, a crumbling watchtower that sits on a ridge between Amalfi and Atrani. Locals will tell you that it was in this spooky overlook that Giovanna and her younger children were murdered – but they are most probably wrong. A more likely spot for the dirty deed would have been in the Norman castle higher up the same ridge that called itself home to the Dukes of Amalfi until the building was dismantled in 1583. To visit both ruins, plan for an easy one-hour walk from the village of **Pontone**, accessible from Amalfi by local bus services.

Locals say the duchess was murdered in the Torre dello Ziro, a crumbling tower overlooking the Duomo

Ravello

If you have had enough of the crowded beaches, scary hairpin bends and are seeking a little refinement, then Ravello is the place for you. Perched 350m (1,150ft) above sea level atop the dramatic Lattari hills overlooking the coast, what it lacks in seaside fun it more than makes up for in breathtaking views. Added to that is fine dining, historic monuments and one of the best hotels in the world, as well as the hugely successful Ravello Festival, which pulls in music lovers and VIP audiences throughout the long summer months.

History

Though often ignored in favour of nearby Amalfi, Ravello is steeped in history. Once a mover and shaker to rival many of its more famous neighbours along the Amalfi Coast, Ravello made its fortune in mercantile trade and at the city's peak – during the 12th and 13th centuries – it boasted four monasteries, a hospital and almost 36,000 denizens. This number has dwindled to the extent that Ravello is little more than a village and its main trade now is tourism. Nevertheless, Ravello's enormous wealth in medieval times has left its mark on the town, with a plethora of fine churches and cloisters.

Following Ravello's rise and fall, it enjoyed popularity as a tourist destination in the 1800s and 1900s, particularly with artists, writers and musicians such as Richard Wagner, who took inspiration from the views from Villa Rufolo when writing *Parsifal*. Other famous visitors include Edward Grieg, E M Forster and Greta Garbo.

Nowadays people visit Ravello by the coach-load, but this does not detract from its sense of serenity. There is always a cool church or a medieval side street to duck into should the hordes descend.

Duomo di Ravello

Ravello Cathedral was built in 1086 under the auspices of the first Bishop of Ravello and is full of artistic treasures. The first is the bronze portal, created in Constantinople in 1179 and shipped over. There are two beautifully decorated pulpits in the central aisle and charming mosaics depicting Jonah and the whale. Other delights include a phial of St Pantaleon's blood in the eponymous chapel. If you are in Ravello in the height of summer, you may get a chance to see the blood in miraculous liquid form.

Piazza del Duomo.
Tel: 089 858 311; www.chiesaravello.it.
Open: Church daily 8.30am–1pm, 3–8pm. Museum Apr–Oct daily 9.30am–1pm, 3–7pm; Nov–Mar Sat, Sun 9.30am–1pm, 3–7pm. Admission charge.

Ravello Festival

There have been music festivals in various guises for many years, but the Ravello Festival – more a summer programme of musical events than an actual festival – is the organising body that brings together events such as art and dance, as well as music to the city throughout the summer months. Each year the festival takes a theme (2009's was courage) to link the various performances.

Fondazione Ravello – Sala Frau, Viale Richard Wagner 5. Tel: 089 858 360; www.ravellofestival.com. Festival performances take place Apr–Sept.

Villa Cimbrone

Records of Villa Cimbrone date back to around the 11th century, the golden age of Ravello. It was originally owned by a Roman patrician family before passing into the hands of other noble dynasties. What make the villa so special are its gardens with panoramic views from the Belvedere Cimbrone. The villa itself is now a prestigious hotel.

Via Santa Chiara 26. Tel: 089 857 459; www.villacimbrone.com. Open: daily 9am–30min before sunset. Admission charge.

Villa Rufolo

Villa Rufolo is a splendid garden estate and shares much in common with Villa Cimbrone. It was here that Wagner was inspired to write his great opera and the villa evokes his memory with concerts under the auspices of the Ravello Festival. If you are not a music lover, but more a green-fingered type, Villa Rufolo's gardens are a treat. Dating back to the 13th century, when the villa was built for the enormously wealthy Rufolo family, they were redesigned in 1851 by Scotsman Francis Reid, who found them in a forlorn state. You can now visit them in all their splendour.

Piazza del Duomo 1.
Tel: 089 857 096 (tourist office); www.villarufolo.it. Open: daily summer 9am–8pm (5pm on concert days); winter 9am–5pm. Admission charge.

An orchestra in full swing at the Ravello Festival

Tour: the perfect Amalfi Coast drive

The Amalfi Coast is made to be driven, preferably by someone else. So bad is the traffic during the high season that it is often described as Europe's most picturesque car park. If you plan on driving the route, arrive early or late in the season, being sure to time it well, as most facilities, hotels, shops and restaurants close between November and February.

Allow 8 hours.

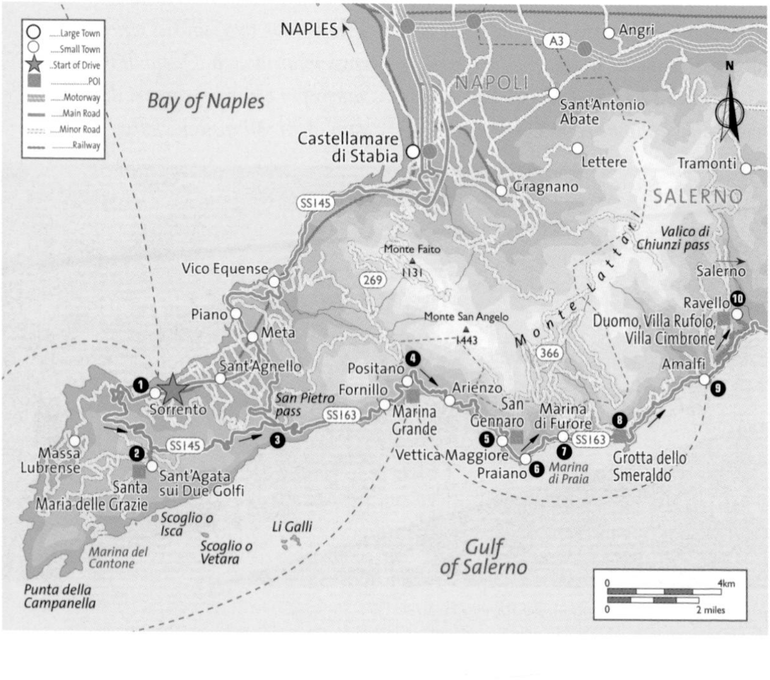

A drive along the Amalfi Coast isn't cheap, especially if you choose to do it yourself. Non-resident parking spaces are few and far between and cost a minimum of €25 per day during high season, so plan your stops economically. Drivers will need to have a head for heights, quick reflexes and should be sure to use the helpful mirrors set up at every sharp corner along the road – and there are a lot of them.

If you prefer, you can trust your wallet, your time and your life to the expert bus drivers that traverse the route every day. In many cases, planned tours offer a hop-on, hop-off service that allows you to spend as much time as you want in any town along the coast.

This tour should take eight hours if you include stops for lunch, sunbathing, shopping and a chance to rest your legs. It begins in Sorrento at the Nastro Azzuro road (SS145). The road exits Sorrento to the west, but will eventually go eastbound, following a series of hairpin turns via Sant'Agata sui Due Golfi.

1 Sorrento

Begin your tour in Sorrento, at the western end of the Sorrento Peninsula. Be sure not to miss the Duomo, Villa Fiorentino and various museums dedicated to chronicling Sorrento's cultural past. If at all possible, try to avoid the busy port: during high season it can sometimes resemble Benidorm with its proliferation of 'English' pubs serving plates of egg and chips to bright-red package tourists.

Drive west out of town, using the SS145. Your drive will continue along this road until you reach San Pietro where you should follow directions for the SS163.

2 Sant'Agata sui Due Golfi

A nondescript village that was once a favourite summer resort during the

Santa Maria Assunta, Positano

18th and 19th centuries. Stop to visit the 17th-century church of **Santa Maria delle Grazie** (*Open: daily 8am–1pm, 5–7pm*), featuring an immense multicoloured inlaid marble altar. Gourmets should make a reservation at the Michelin-starred **Don Alfonso restaurant** (*Corso Sant'Agata 13. Tel: 081 878 0026*) for its divine interpretations of local dishes. All of the garden produce is organic. The *boccadoro* (bream) comes highly recommended.

3 Between Sant'Agata and Positano: Li Galli and the San Pietro pass

The 14km (8¾-mile) stretch between Sant'Agata and Positano is one of the area's most difficult to manoeuvre. Steinbeck and his wife certainly

Marina di Furore

thought so when they 'lay clutched in each other's arms, weeping hysterically', as their driver – in his typically Italian fashion – constantly took his eyes off the road while behind the wheel of the car to talk about the region's history.

Just off the coast are three islands, known in days of old as the home of the deadly sirens, who lured mariners to their deaths with their song. Today, the islands are known as Li Galli and can be explored if you charter a boat from the docks at Positano.

4 Positano

This popular seaside resort is a great place to rest your legs. The main beach, Marina Grande, isn't exactly the most comfortable of locations to pick up a tan, filled as it is with grey pebbles, but the activity from the cafés that line the shore is addictive to watch. Colourful boats pull up to the docks throughout the day, depositing their catches straight into the hands of the numerous restaurant owners and chefs who feed their mouthwatering dishes to thousands of tourists every day.

For shopping, be sure to head for the Piazza dei Mulini and the Via dei Mulini, a narrow street that runs off the beach past the church of **Santa Maria Assunta** (*Open: daily 8am–noon, 4–7pm. Tel: 089 875 480; www.chiesapositano.com*). For other sites, *see p133.*

5 Vettica Maggiore

This tiny village offers a beautiful beach and one of the coast's most picturesque churches, San Gennaro. The view from the square outside the church is simply stunning, providing perfect photo opportunities back to Positano and the rocky coast beyond.

6 Praiano

A mini-Positano with a fishing cove lying just to the east of the main part of town in the Marina di Praia. The local beach is absolutely tiny, stuck between a couple of high rock walls that allow room for only a few bar-restaurants and residences.

7 Marina di Furore

Even smaller than any of the villages previously mentioned, the Marina di Furore was recently restored with funds provided by the Campanian government. A new bar-restaurant, cinema archive, cultural centre, paper-

A slice of heaven: the Amalfi coastline

making museum and herbarium have been opened under the auspices of the **Ecomuseo** complex.
Hours are erratic, so be sure to call ahead for details on 089 830 781.

8 Grotta dello Smeraldo

Amalfi's answer to Capri's famous Blue Grotto is this emerald-hued cove, located two-thirds of the way between Positano and Amalfi. A car park above the cave sits near the entrance to a lift that takes you down to a series of rowing boats that plunge under the tiny entrance. While it's not as impressive as its more famous sister grotto in Capri, it's certainly cheaper. See if you can find the profile of former dictator Benito Mussolini formed by the shadow of a stalagmite.

9 Amalfi

This former marine powerhouse may have lost some of its lustre since the 11th century, but there's still plenty to see and do. Another good place for a bite to eat and a bit of shopping, details of the better-known local sites can be found on *pp134–5.*

10 Ravello

Ravello has drawn great artists and writers to its aristocratic old town for the best part of a century. Beginning with Richard Wagner (honoured in a music festival each summer), everyone from Franz Liszt to Virginia Woolf spent time in the romantic palazzi and hotels that dot the town. D H Lawrence is even said to have written large parts of *Lady Chatterley's Lover* in the now-defunct Hotel Rufolo. A great place to spend the night, Ravello has plenty of other sites to explore, including the Duomo, Villa Rufolo and Villa Cimbrone to name a few, *see pp138–9.*

Getting away from it all

Getting out of Naples is something all residents look forward to. While they could never think of living anywhere else, all that smog, traffic and humanity are bound to get on your nerves at some time. Luckily, the countryside surrounding the city is filled with countless rural opportunities to while away lazy summer days or fill up on culture.

CASERTA

Caserta was an insignificant little town from its founding in the 12th century until the 1750s when the first Bourbon King Charles decided to select the area as the location of his countryside residence. Situated 20km (12½ miles) north of Naples, Caserta provided a quiet spot where Charles could flee the threat of marauding Saracens and the eruptions of Vesuvius while satisfying his passion for hunting.

Reggia di Caserta (Palazzo Reale)

Built around four courtyards, the Reggia has 1,790 windows in 1,200 rooms, of which only a fraction are open to the public. The whole place cost around six million ducats to build and is probably the finest example of Neapolitan Baroque architecture in Italy.

Salone delle Guardie di Corpo

This salon is the ultimate in Bourbon family self-love, filled with painted scenes taken from the lives of the Farnese family. A bust of Ferdinand I on the mantelpiece is attributed to Antonio Canova. The room next to it (the **Sala di Alessandro**) gets its name from the fresco showing Alexander the Great's marriage to Roxana. The terrace outside was used by reigning monarchs and their families to greet the commoners with a 'royal wave'.

IL PARCO

Luigi Vanvitelli not only designed the massive Reggia di Caserta (Palazzo Reale), he was also in charge of landscaping the immense gardens surrounding the palace – and what a job he made of it. One of the last examples of a regimented garden in the Italian style, the central axis is designed on descending levels, each littered with pools, fountains and ornamental sculptures. The *pièce de résistance* is the **Grande Cascata** waterfall. Almost 80m (260ft) high, the Cascata (also known as the Fountain of Diana) acts as the park's central feature. Located next to this is the **English Garden**, one of the first of its kind in Italy. Landscaping work on the English Garden began in 1768 after the idea was suggested to Queen Maria Carolina by her very close 'friend' Lord Hamilton.

Eighteenth-century Royal Apartments

The Halberdiers Hall connects the upper vestibule with the Royal Apartments. The ceiling is decorated with a fresco painted by Domenico Mondo in 1785, entitled *The Triumph of the Bourbon Arms*. The furniture and decoration of the rooms act as a veritable museum, documenting the development of craftsmanship from the Rococo period to the Neoclassical.

Appartamento Vecchio

Each of the first four rooms in this series of apartments is dedicated to the four seasons, beginning with *primavera* (spring). The walls of the *estate* (summer) room are covered in San Leucio silk and topped off with a priceless chandelier made from Murano glass, while the *autumno* dining room has stunning frescoes of Bacchus and Ariadne.

Sala del Trono (Throne Room)

This large salon was decorated by Gaetano Genovese in 1844. The room is lit by 14 Bohemian glass and bronze lamps and has a throne of carved and gilded wood.

Ferdinand II's bedchamber lies close to the throne room. The adjoining bathroom and study belonged to Joaquin Murat, brother-in-law to Napoleon and King of Naples from 1808 to 1816. The bedchamber is in the French Empire style, filled with mahogany furniture. Note Murat's initials carved into the chairs.

La Biblioteca (Library)

The library houses a collection of over 10,000 volumes. Next to the library is a Nativity scene containing over 1,200 figures made by 18th-century craftsmen. The clothing on all of the figures was made by the queen and her ladies-in-waiting.

Museo dell'Opera

Students of architecture will love the displays and records containing documents and plans tracing the history of the palace's construction.

Via Douhet 2. Tel: Reggia 0823 277 380. Museum dell'Opera 0823 448 084; www.reggiadicaserta.beniculturali.it. Open: Reggia Wed–Mon 8.30am–7.30pm. Museum Wed–Mon 8.30am–6pm. Park Tue–Sun 8.30am–1hr before sunset. Admission charge.

Getting there

By bus

CTP (*Tel: 081 700 1111; www.ctpn.it*) runs from Piazza Garibaldi in Naples to Caserta and Capua. Look for buses marked *per autostrada*: these services take the motorway and cut journey times in half.

By car

Take the A1 motorway from Naples, exiting at Caserta Sud.

By train

Frequent services run to Caserta from Naples' Stazione Centrale. The journey takes about 30 minutes, followed by a 5-minute walk to the Reggia di Caserta.

PAESTUM

The ruins of Paestum date back to 600 BC when Greeks from Sybaris founded a large town on the bank of the River Sele. The colony, known as Poseidonia, featured a traditional grid-pattern layout of massive temples, and a vast *agora* (market) testifying to the area's prosperity. Don't miss the adjoining **Archaeological Museum**, which has some excellent displays of Greek sculpture.

Roman Paestum

Poseidonia became a Roman colony in 273 BC and was renamed Paestum. Paestum took to Romanisation easily, and flourished briefly until the Second Punic War brought soldiers carrying malaria into the city gates. Residents bravely battled the disease throughout the 1st century AD, until it finally took its toll and the city was abandoned.

Agora

This is located south of the main entrance to the site on a plateau. Excavations underneath revealed two Greek structures, the **Underground Sacellum** and the **Ekklesiasterion**. Built in 470 BC, the Ekklesiasterion was the government centre of Poseidonia. Citizens would gather to pass laws and elect local magistrates. When the Romans arrived, democracy was thrown out the window and the structure was filled in.

The Sacellum was more religious in tone, built to house the symbolic sepulchre of the town's hero. It was buried as a 'lucky charm' or shrine to protect the city from evil.

The Forum

A Roman addition, the Forum was used as the city's public square. One of the most complete ancient structures in Italy, the Forum contains an amphitheatre, town treasury, Italic Temple and a number of *tabernae* (stores).

Via Magna Grecia 917. Tel: 082 811 023; www.paestumsites.it. Open: Site daily 9am–1hr before sunset. Museum daily 9am–7pm. Closed 1st & 3rd Mon of the month. Admission charge.

Getting there

By bus

Hourly services are run by **CSTP** (*Tel: 089 487 111; www.cstp.it*) from Salerno's Piazza della Concordia. For bus services to Salerno, *see opposite*.

By car

Take the A3 motorway south from Naples to Salerno. From Salerno, follow the SS18 coast road south to Paestum.

By train

The Naples–Reggio–Calabria line from Naples' Stazione Centrale stops at Paestum. The main train station is called Capaccio Scalo. Buses run infrequently from the station to the ruins. Try to board a train stopping at the much smaller Paestum station, ten minutes by foot from the site. Trains run to and from this station less frequently.

SALERNO

Salerno proper owes its roots to the Roman town of Salernum, which was founded on this site in 194 BC. The city didn't hit its stride until the dawn of the Lombards and (especially) the Normans, who made Salerno their capital in 1077.

This boom period didn't fall down until the 13th century, with the rise of the Angevins, who favoured neighbouring Naples as their administrative headquarters. Salernians still haven't really got over this fact and hold bitter feelings for their more prosperous Neapolitan cousins.

Duomo

Dedicated to the town's patron saint, St Matthew, the Duomo dominates the centre of the old city. Built after the Norman conquest of the town in the 11th century, the Duomo was constructed to celebrate victory over the Lombards. Designed in the Romanesque style, the exterior was heavily altered in the 18th century in the Baroque fashion during an era of major post-earthquake reconstruction. Subsequent restorations have reverted to the original Romanesque look, but elements of the 'update' remain.
Piazza Alfano 1. Tel: 089 231 387. Open: daily 7.30am–8pm. Free admission.

Temple of Neptune at the Roman Paestum

Museo Archeologico Provinciale

Situated in the former abbey of San Benedetto, this museum is dedicated to the Etruscan influence on the city. One of the highlights of the collection is a 1st-century bronze head of Apollo, found in the Gulf of Salerno in 1930.
Via San Benedetto 28. Tel: 089 231 135. Open: Tue–Sat 9am–7.30pm, Sun 9am–1pm. Free admission.

Getting there

By bus

SITA (*Tel: 089 386 6711; www.sitabus.it*) runs regular services from Naples' Piazza Municipio.

By car

Salerno is located directly on the A3 motorway 55km (34 miles) south from Naples.

By train

Regular services run on the Naples–Reggio–Calabria line from Naples' Stazione Centrale. Journey time is approximately 45 minutes.

Shopping

Naples may not be a fashion mecca like Milan, but there are still plenty of opportunities to blow your budget. Retailers in the city follow old-fashioned sales methods, with the focus on them serving you, not you helping yourself. With everything from antiques to Armani on sale, opportunities to spend your money abound!

If a shop has display shelves, be sure to ask a shop assistant for help. If you speak Italian, it will help you immeasurably, but don't try out your Neapolitan dialect unless you want to give the shop assistants a giggle! Speak with a Neapolitan accent and you may even be given good customer service.

Shopping hours

Many shops in Naples close for lunch, 1.30–4.30pm. Some clothes and food shops open on Sunday mornings, particularly around Montesanto and Centro Storico. Certain food shops close on Thursday afternoons in winter. The majority of non-food shops close on Monday mornings. Saturday afternoons during summer are also often a no-go time. In August, schedules get thrown out the window as locals abandon the city for their annual holiday.

What to buy

Naples is renowned for a number of items, both edible and not. This town wasn't a courtly capital and artistic headquarters for nothing! Whether you're a bibliophile who loves to collect antiquarian books, a foodie who devours antipasti at every opportunity or a fashionista who loves Italian clothes, then you've come to the right place. Bargains are available all year, but the best deals are found during the sale seasons of January, February and August.

Be sure to try on all items of clothing before you buy them. US and UK sizes printed on the labels often differ greatly from the actual truth, and refund policies are non-existent in almost all Neapolitan shops.

Pickpockets ahead!

To avoid being targeted by Naples' deadly-accurate pickpockets, avoid shopping between the hours of 6pm and 8pm. Workers going home after a long day crowd the streets along with locals out for a stroll, transforming pavements into a mess of elbows and shopping bags. Be sensible; don't keep your wallet in your back pocket or bag behind you.

NAPLES

Antiquarian books and prints

Bowinkel

The most respected dealer of period prints and photographs in town.
Piazza dei Martiri 24, Chiaia.
Tel: 081 764 4344.

Colonnese

Publishers and collectors of works both old and new. Speciality subjects include the arts, magic and history. A great place to find distinctive Neapolitan tarot and playing cards.
Via San Pietro a Maiella 33, Chiaia.
Tel: 081 459 858; www.colonnese.it

Books

Liberia Feltrinelli

The biggest bookshop in Naples. Go downstairs to find works in English. Theatre and concert bookings are available on the first floor.
Piazza dei Martiri/Via Santa Caterina a Chiaia 23, Chiaia.
Tel: 081 240 5411.

Ceramics

Ceramics Spagnuolo

Ceramics both authentic and reproduction are on offer at this Aladdin's cave of a shop, packed with examples of everything from simple souvenirs to the finest Capodimonte.
Via Benedetto Croce 55.
Tel: 081 552 1102.

Department stores

Coin

Set in the swish Vomero neighbourhood, you can find a good selection of beauty products, clothing and household goods.
Via Scarlatti 86–100.
Tel: 081 578 0111; www.coin.it

Fashion

Amina Rubinacci

Dubbed 'Queen of Wool' by Paris designers, Amina and her daughter Federica – who creates a younger collection – produce timelessly elegant fashion.
Via dei Mille 16, Chiaia.
Tel: 081 413 048; www.aminarubinacci.com

Eddy Monetti

Conservative yet well-crafted pieces that are both timeless and fashionable. The quality is impeccably high. So are the prices. Womenswear is located a few doors down in the Piazzetta Santa Caterina.
Via dei Mille 45, Chiaia.
Tel: 081 407 064; www.eddymonetti.it

Maxi Ho

The best selection of fashion-forward and avant-garde pieces for women in Naples. A far cry from the traditionally tailored clothing available at most other boutiques.
Via Nisco 20, Chiaia.
Tel: 081 414 721.

Melinoi
Elegant ladies consider this boutique their secret treasure. All of the items on sale are unique, hailing from designers based across Europe.
Via Benedetto Croce 34.
Tel: 081 552 1204.

Food and drink

Antiche Delizie
The best mozzarella in town. Also the best meat, cheese, preserves and antipasti. Wines and fresh pasta dishes are also on offer.
Via Pasquale Scura 14, Toledo.
Tel: 081 551 3088.

Jewellery

Arte in Oro
Fabulous copies of original Roman jewellery. Antique items are also available.
Via B Croce 20, Centro Storico.
Tel: 081 551 6980.

Ascione
Exclusive pieces made by local craftsmen.
19 Piazzetta Matilde Serao.
Tel: 081 421 1111; www.ascione.it

Shoes and leather

Fratelli Tramontano
Neapolitan craftsmanship in the form of fine, handmade shoes and bags. Expensive, but worth every cent.
Via Chiaia 142–143, Royal.
Tel: 081 414 837;
www.tramontano.it

AMALFI

Antichi Sapori d'Amalfi
Limoncello and fruit liqueurs aplenty. All are locally produced in small batches and are extremely potent.
Piazza Duomo 39. Tel: 089 872 062; www.antichisaporidamalfi.it

Pasticceria Andrea Pansa 1830
Wonderful pastry shop specialising in anything flavoured with lemons.
Piazza del Duomo 40. Tel: 089 871 065; www.pasticceriapansa.it

La Scuderia del Duca
Amalfi's best handmade paper shop. Available by the sheet or in books and reams.
Largo Cesareo Console 8.
Tel: 089 872 976; www.carta-amalfi.it

CAPRI

Designer shops line **Via Vittorio Emanuele** and **Via Camerelle**. Big names include Gucci, Fendi and Ferragamo. For something a little more native, try the following options:

Carthusia
Probably Capri's most famous shop, Carthusia creates and blends perfumes using local flowers. Many celebrities are counted among the shop's clientele.
Viale Matteotti 2D.
Tel: 081 837 0368; www.carthusia.com

La Conchiglia
A local publisher with a catalogue of books about Capri's history and

residents. Some of the works have been translated into English.
Via Camerelle 18.
Tel: 081 837 8199;
www.laconchigliacapri.com

Limoncello di Capri
The shop where it all started. If you're looking for the best example of the local liqueur, then come to the place where they first created it.
Via Listrieri 25A. Tel: 081 837 3059;
www.limoncello.com

SORRENTO

Apreda
Delicious cheeses and regional vintages are served at this local food shop featuring the finest in organic and local produce.
Via Tasso 27. Tel: 081 878 1334;
www.caseificioapreda.it

Gargiulo & Jannuzzi
In operation since the 19th century, this marquetry furniture manufacturer is probably the finest in Sorrento. Visit the workshop to see incredible examples of woodworking and craftwork.
Piazza Tasso 1. Tel: 081 878 1041;
www.gargiulo-jannuzzi.it

Salvatore Gargiulo
Sorrento's best furniture workshop, specialising in marquetry and wooden inlay which is famous throughout the region.
Via Fuoro 33. Tel: 081 878 2420;
www.gargiuloinlaid.it

Ceramics shop, Ravello

The markets of Old Napoli

One of Naples' most pleasurable shopping experiences is a visit to a market. Pulsing with energy, this is definitely not a challenge for the faint of heart. If you thought that the Harrods Christmas sales could get ugly, then you have never tried to snag a bargain in this town. To tackle the markets effectively, banish all thoughts of order and queuing. If you see something you like, then grab it before someone else does. If there is a long wait, take matters into your own hands by jostling for position and don't be afraid to holler when it's your turn to be served. Even little old ladies get in on the act – in fact, they use their perceived frailness to their advantage! So keep your wallet firmly hidden, check your credit cards at the door (trust me, you won't be needing them) and prepare yourself for a fight. Round one begins now.

Bancarelle a San Pasquale
Edible goodies are sold along Via San Pasquale and Via Carducci. Things to wear are available in stalls on Via Imbriani. Good for fish, fruit, vegetables, underwear and cheap jewellery.
Via Carducci, Via Imbriani and Via San Pasquale, Chiaia. Open: Mon–Wed, Fri, Sat 8am–2pm. Closed: Aug. Bus: C25. Tram: 1, 4.

Fiera Antiquaria Napoletana
A treasure trove of antiques both real and fake. If one of Naples' crumbling villas is emptying their stock out, then chances are you'll find it here.
Villa Comunale, Chiaia. Open: 8am–2pm last Sun of the month and occasional Sat. Closed: Aug. Bus: C25. Tram: 1, 4.

Mercatino di Antignano
The best place for things for the home. Tons of kitchenware, linens and towels at cut-rate prices. Goods are both second-hand and end-of-the-line markdowns.
Between Via Mario Fiore and Piazza degli Artisti, Vomero. Open: Mon–Sat 8am–2pm. Closed: Aug. Metro: Medaglie d'Oro. Bus: R1.

Mercatino di Poggioreale
Shoes, shoes and more shoes. Check for quality before you buy.
Via M di Caramanico, off Via Nuova, Poggioreale. Open: Mon, Fri–Sun 7am–1pm. Closed: Aug. Bus: C61, C62. Tram: 1, 4.

Mercatino di Posillipo

More clothes, shoes and bags. The early bird definitely gets the fake Fendi.
Viale Virgilio, Posillipo. Open: Thur 8am–2pm. Closed: Aug. Bus: C27.

Mercatino di Resina

A massive flea market packed with goods taken from homes across the Bay area. You want a used accordion? They've got it! An original pair of opera glasses? Try selecting from six possible stalls! How about a couple of centuries-old linen nighties? Why not three? Situated in Ercolano, a visit here makes a great day out when combined with a visit to the site of Herculaneum.
Via Pugliano, Ercolano. Open: daily 8am–1pm. Closed: Aug. Circumvesuviana rail to Ercolano.

Mercato delle Pulci

Old knick-knacks, small furnishings and ceramics. Most of it is trash, but you'll occasionally find the odd gem or two.
Via de Roberto, Poggioreale. Open: Sun 8am–1pm. Closed: Aug. Bus: 191.

La Pignasecca

One of the city's oldest markets, packed with fish, vegetables, deli nibbles, perfumes, clothes, linens and kitchenware. Nothing is five-star, but it's the atmosphere that makes it all worth it.
Via Pignasecca. Open: daily 8am–1pm. Funicular: Montesanto to Montesanto (see pp68–9 for details)*. Metro: Montesanto. Bus: 24, 105, R1.*

You can find almost anything at a Naples market

Entertainment

When it comes to entertainment, Naples shouldn't fail to fulfil all your expectations – and more. You may have to book well ahead for some of the big-ticket offerings at the San Carlo, but you won't be disappointed if a street-side serenade is all you can afford. The city that brought us commedia dell'arte *and the movie magic of Sophia Loren is culturally alive. From visually vibrant art to momentous music, Naples has it all.*

Theatres

Bellini

A sumptuous theatre that stages prose, musicals, dance and concerts. Plays are usually performed in Italian.
Via Conte di Ruvo 14–19.
Tel: 081 549 1266;
www.teatrobellini.it

Elicantropo

Intimate, 40-seat fringe theatre with a focus on new works. Like all fringe theatres, productions can be hit or miss.
Vico Gerolomini 3.
Tel: 081 296 640;
www.teatroelicantropo.com

Mercadante

A beautiful theatre that has been staging performances since 1779. The acoustics are uniformly awful.
Piazza Municipio 1.
Tel: 081 551 0336;
www.teatrostabilenapoli.it

Le Nuvole

Kids' shows in a theatre situated in the heart of the Edenlandia amusement park.
Viale Kennedy 26. Tel: 081 239 5653;
www.lenuvole.com

Teatro di San Carlo

Naples' *pièce de résistance.* Second only to Milan's La Scala as a home to opera. The San Carlo ballet company also performs on this stage.
Via San Carlo 98F. Tel: 081 797 2331;
www.teatrosancarlo.it

Teatro Nuovo

A modern theatre built over the site of one of the city's oldest theatres. New and international theatre is the focus.
Via Montecalvario 16.
Tel: 081 406 062;
www.nuovoteatronuovo.it

Teatro Trianon

Naples' newest addition to the theatre scene is this performance space dedicated to traditional Neapolitan

art forms. While you probably won't understand the dialects used, it's a slice of local life you have to see to appreciate.
Piazza Calenda 9. Tel: 081 225 8285; www.teatrotrianon.it

Summer arts festivals

When the summer weather gets too hot to bear, concerts move outdoors. Teatro di San Carlo also has summer programmes in Piazza del Plebiscito, such as 2009's celebration of Verdi. Check website for details. A few festivals to take note of:

accordi@DISACCORDI
Summer film festival showing international independent movies under the stars.
Parco del Poggio, Viale del Poggio di Capodimonte. Tel: 081 549 1838; www.accordiedisaccordi.com

Un'estate al MADRe
Throughout the summer months, MADRe hosts a series of open-air events from the world of music, dance, cinema and theatre.
Via Settembrini 79. Tel: 081 1931 3016; www.museomadre.com

Festival d'Oltremare
July and August see dance, music and theatre come to the Arena Flegrea for al fresco performances in a stunning setting.
Arena Flegrea (entrance Via Terracina). Tel: 081 426 555; www.napoliteatrofestival.it

Festival Ville Vesuviane
Dance, music and theatre are staged in 18th-century villas in the so-called Miglio d'Oro along the Neapolitan coastline.
Villa Campolieto, Corso Resina 283, Ercolano. Tel: 081 732 2134; www.villevesuviane.net

Galleries

The Neapolitan modern art scene has seen something of a revival since 1993. Under former mayor Antonio Bassolino, the city commissioned a number of public works specifically for the new underground system. Art galleries

A souvenir mask symbolises the city's love of the arts

have sprouted up to accommodate this new-found interest. Some of the better galleries include:

Changing Role

Less arty and more focused on the creative and colourful, this gallery space is less concerned with an artist's reputation than with the brightness of the end results – the more vivid the image, the more likely you'll find it here.
Via Chiatamone 26. Tel: 081 1957 5958; www.changingrole.com

Galleria Scognamiglio

Personal exhibitions by Italian and foreign artists.
Via M d'Ayala 6. Tel: 081 400 871; www.mimmoscognamiglio.com

Raucci Santamaria

A superlative gallery specialising in design and applied arts. The best of Europe is represented in well-curated shows.
Corso Amedeo di Savoia 190. Tel: 081 744 3645; www.raucciesantamaria.com

Studio Trisorio

Founded in 1974, this is still one of the most active galleries in town, dealing in contemporary international art.
Riviera di Chiaia 215. Tel: 081 414 306; www.studiotrisorio.com

T293

This gallery is located in two separate spaces and focuses on recent works from up-and-coming European and American artists.
Via dei Tribunali 293. Tel: 081 295 882; www.t293.it

Teatro di San Carlo

Cinemas

Naples may be home to Sophia Loren, but, unlike her, no cinema-goer will ever learn anything but Italian, since almost all films are dubbed. Look for the letters VO (*versione originale*) for English-language screenings.

Filangieri Multisala

Predominantly Italian and international commercial films, though some indie movies too.
Via Filangieri 43–47. Tel: 081 251 2408.

Modernissimo

An arthouse cinema with children's films, restored classics and European oddities.
Via Cisterna dell'Olio 59.
Tel: 081 580 0254; www.modernissimo.it

Plaza

Enjoy the output of Hollywood in its original language on Tuesday evenings. All other evenings feature dubbed soundtracks.
Via Kerbaker 85, Vomero.
Tel: 081 556 3555.

Bars and clubs

Around Midnight

As you might expect from the name, jazz is the main player in this live music venue. However, world music and blues also get a look-in and there are even poetry reading nights.
Via Bonito 32A. Open: Tue–Sun 8pm–1am. Tel: 081 558 2834; www.aroundmidnight.it

Farinella

The renowned architect Scognamiglio had his hand in the renovation of Farinella, with bare bricks, mirrors and marble. Popular with youngish Neapolitan professionals, this is a good place to kick off the evening.
Via Alabradieri 10. Open: Mon–Sat 7pm–1am. Tel: 081 423 0710.

Intra Moenia

Situated in one of the most popular squares for late-night drinking, Intra Moenia offers friendly service at its city garden tables. Sip on a *finocchietto* (fennel liqueur) as you rub shoulders with the locals.
Piazza Bellini 70. Open: daily 10am–2am Tel: 081 290 720.

Miami Bar Room

A strange mixture of minimalism and kitsch that somehow works, this bar and lounge has a bar to be seen in and little nooks perfect for secret trysts.
Via Morghen 68C. Open: Wed–Sun 10pm–4am. Tel: 081 229 8332; www.miamibarroom.it

S'move Light Bar

A stalwart on the Neapolitan nightlife scene. DJ sessions, great cocktails and S'move's own birthday parties are held here.
Vico dei Sospiri 10. Open: daily 7pm–2am. Tel: 081 764 5813; www.smove-lab.net

Il Solo

House, dance and electronica are on the menu at this club. Put on your glad rags and get dancing.
Via Giuseppe Ferrigni 19. Open: Tue–Sun 10pm–3am. Tel: 081 764 7420.

Tempio di Bacco

One of the most original bars in town. A wine bar, but there's also a small menu of first courses. The ambience is neon blue with neoclassical busts and statues. An acquired taste.
Vico San Domenico Maggiore 12. Open: daily 4pm–2am. Tel: 081 294 354.

Children

Naples is a child-friendly city in name only. While perfect strangers will dote all over your little angels at every opportunity, the streets are certainly not made for their entertainment. If you were ever told by your parents about the days when kicking around a ball was all that was needed for hours of entertainment then you can see it in practice in Neapolitan streets.

Beaches

City beaches are decidedly unclean and should be avoided at all costs. Your best bet is to head out of town to the Amalfi Coast or to the outlying islands. The beaches here are small and rocky, and you will have to keep watch on your children at all times.

Funfair

Edenlandia is a traditional funfair with a host of ageing thrill-rides. Your kids will love it.
Viale Kennedy, Fuorigrotta. Tel: 081 239 409; www.edenlandia.it. Open: Apr, May Tue–Fri 2–8pm, Sat, Sun 10.30am–midnight; Jun–Sept Tue–Fri 5pm–midnight, Sat, Sun 10.30am–midnight; Oct–Mar Sat, Sun 10.30am–midnight.

Museums

Few museums offer the type of hands-on displays kids know and love. Some of the more interesting displays from a child's perspective are at the Musei Interdipartimentali for fossils and stuffed animals, the Nativity crib in the Certosa-Museo di San Martino (*see p67*), the medieval works and fortifications in the Castel dell'Ovo (*see p33*) and the dungeons of the Castel Nuovo (*see pp33–4*). Of note is the **Città delle Scienze** (*Via Coroglio 104. Tel: 081 242 0024; www.cittadellescienze.it. Open: Tue–Sat 9am–5pm, Sun 10am–7pm*), a child-friendly museum of attractions, many of which are hands-on. Also inside is a Planetarium with showings throughout the day. The subterranean options around the city are great for children who love Indiana Jones, while the catacombs offer an eerie thrill. The aquarium, situated in a park and close to the seafront, is another option.

Outside the city, your best bets are the ancient ruins of Pompeii, the sulphurous crater of Vesuvius and the Pietarsa railway museum (*see p90*) – even if you aren't a fan of trains, it's still worth a visit.

Public parks

For a spot of outdoor play in the heart of town, take your children to the Villa Comunale or Villa Floridiana – but they won't feature many of the playground options your kids may be searching for. For the usual set of swings and slides, you'll have to head further afield to the **Parco del Poggio** in the northwest of town.

Shopping

If you need children's clothes while in Naples, then department stores and markets are your best resource. To keep your kids occupied while you do the shopping, head over to Liberia Feltrinelli's basement (*see p149*), which contains the largest selection of English reading material in Naples.

Children playing in the Villa Comunale park

Sport and leisure

Italians are passionate about sport, especially football. Tickets to major matches can be like gold dust but are well worth the trip, if only to see the carnival of activity that goes on at every match. There are plenty of opportunities to participate in sports in Naples. From bowling and sailing to water sports and tennis, there are facilities to suit all tastes.

SPECTATOR SPORTS

Football

Italian football is like a religion and Neapolitans worship their local team, SSC Napoli, now settled in Serie A after years of disappointment. **Stadio San Paolo** is where all the action takes place, and matches are played on alternate Sundays between September and June. Kick-off can be any time between 2.30pm and 4.30pm. Check the time when you buy your ticket. Tickets for all matches (when available) can be bought at the club's main outlet, Azzuro Service.

Azzuro Service *Via F Galeoata 17, Fuorigrotta. Tel: 081 593 4001.*

Stadio San Paolo *Piazzale Tecchio, Fuorigrotta. Tel: 081 593 3223.*

SPORTING ACTIVITIES

Bowling

Bowling Oltremare

A 20-lane bowling alley located next to the zoo and Edenlandia funfair. Ping-pong tables are also available for hire by the hour.

Viale Kennedy 12, Fuorigrotta. Tel: 081 624 444. Open: Sun–Thur 9am–2am, Fri, Sat 9am–4am.

Gyms

Athenae

Featuring the usual gym equipment, as well as aerobics classes, bicycles, weights and martial arts. There is also a Turkish bath, sauna, bar and squash court.

Via dei Mille 16, Chiaia. Tel: 081 407 334. Open: Jul–Aug Mon–Fri 8am–10.30pm; Oct–Jun Mon–Fri 8am–10.30pm, Sat 9am–6pm, Sun 9am–12.30pm. Closed: Sept.

Bodyguard

Weights, bicycles, running machines and a sauna. Aerobics and dance classes are also on offer.

Via Torrione San Martino 45, Vomero. Tel: 081 558 4551. Open: Mon–Fri 8.30am–11pm, Sat 10am–7pm. Closed: 2 weeks in Aug.

Jogging

There are no official jogging tracks in the city. Popular locations for a run include the seafront from Castel dell'Ovo to Mergellina, the upper reaches of Via Petrarca, the roads around Capo Posillipo and the gardens surrounding the Museo di Capodimonte.

Swimming pools

Collana

A city-owned pool measuring 25m × 8m (82 × 26ft). Admission includes access to the sundeck and deck chairs.
Via Rossini, Vomero. Tel: 081 560 0907. Open: Jul, Aug Tue–Sat 10am–2pm, Sun 9am–2.30pm.

Scandone

Another public swimming pool for the masses. Under-12s get in for half-price.
Viale dei Giochi del Mediterraneo, Fuorigrotta. Tel: 081 570 2636. Open: Jul, Aug daily 9am–7pm.

Tennis

Tennis Club Napoli

Elegant club in Chiaia with lovely clubhouse and pool, not to mention the clay courts. Lessons available.
Viale Dohrn, Villa Comunale. Tel: 081 761 4656; www.tennisclubnapoli.it

Tennis San Domenico

Five floodlit clay courts located under a flyover. Racquets are available free of charge. A separate gym for weight training and aerobics adjoins the club.
Via San Domenico 64, Vomero Alto. Tel: 081 645 660. Open: Mon–Fri 8am–10pm, Sat 8am–7pm, Sun 8am–2pm.

Watch SSC Napoli at the Stadio San Paolo

Food and drink

Neapolitan cuisine is based on the three Ps: pizza, pasta and pomodoro *(tomato). While living next to Vesuvius certainly has its drawbacks, one of the main benefits is the fact that the entire region of Campania is extremely fertile. The volcanic ash has transformed the soil into a rich resource for diverse agriculture, and some of Italy's finest fruits and vegetables can be found on farms throughout the area.*

Glossary of food and drink

Carne al Ragù: A typical Sunday meal of meat rolls served in a tomato sauce.

Casatiello: A traditional country-style pie, made at Easter and filled with a salami, cheese and egg stuffing.

Cheeses and dairy produce: The best local cheese is mozzarella, which was originally made from buffalo milk. *Fiordilatte* and *treccia di mozzarella* (made from cow's milk) are excellent when served with tomatoes and basil. There are many types of *provolone* and *scamorza* cheeses (stuffed and smoked), depending on their origin. Fresh *ricotta* is used for both savouries and sweet pastries. Grated parmesan is often used to flavour pasta dishes.

Coffee: Neapolitan coffee is lighter than espresso and tastes good even when reheated. The coffee is made in a typical Neapolitan coffee maker consisting of two metal cylinders (one with a spout) and a central container to hold finely ground roast coffee.

Frutti di Mare: Seafood served with spaghetti or risotto. It can be fried or grilled when prepared and is usually made up of all different kinds of seafood fished from along the coast.

Parmagiana di Melanzane: Layers of aubergines, tomato sauce, mozzarella, grated parmesan and basil. Courgettes may also be used.

Pasta e Fagioli: A simple dish of pasta and beans.

Pastries: Typical local delicacies include *sfogliatelle* (pastries filled with *ricotta*, sugar and candied fruit), *pastiera* (a special Easter or Christmas cake), *struffoli* (pastries with honey and fruit, usually served at Christmas) and *zeppole* (light doughnuts served during the feast of San Giuseppe).

Pesce all'Acqua Pazza: Fresh fish cooked in water with tomatoes, garlic and parsley.

Sartù di Riso: A rice mould served with garnishes.

Spaghetti con le Vongole: A typical first course of spaghetti with fresh clams.

The sauce can be based either on olive oil or on tomato with parsley.

Wines and drinks: The white *lacrima christi* wine, made for centuries by monks on the slopes of Vesuvius, goes well with fish dishes. *Greco di tufo* is another good possibility, while *limoncello* is a locally produced lemon-flavoured liqueur.

LIMONCELLO

About 100 years ago, a Caprese vintner decided that something had to be done about the island's abundance of lemons. The result: *limoncello*. Today, this sweet lemon-flavoured liqueur is Campania's favourite post-meal tipple and holiday souvenir. While you can buy the stuff on almost every street corner in the region, die-hards will often insist on purchasing it at its source on the island of Capri. **Limoncello di Capri** (*see p151*) is the ancestral home of the luscious lemony liqueur, but producers in Amalfi and Sorrento also whip up some delightful concoctions – even if the bottles they offer differ from the original recipe.

Where to eat

Food is an important feature in the daily life of your typical Neapolitan. As such, there is a plethora of high-quality restaurants to choose from – as long as you like Italian cuisine. If at first glance a dining spot seems run down and cramped, you shouldn't let that dissuade you. Menus may be in dialect or dishes named after a close family relation, but you can easily overcome the problems of translation by taking a look at what others around you are eating. If you like the look of something, point to it when the waiter approaches. The results will invariably tantalise your taste buds to the point of saying 'That's *amore*!'

Luscious *limoncello*

Meal prices

Prices at Italian restaurants can vary widely. Prices in this guide are subject to fluctuation and should only be used as a rough guide. The following refer to a two-course dinner for one person without drinks.

★	under €30
★★	€30–€50
★★★	€50–€65
★★★★	over €65

Enjoy an authentic Neapolitan pizza

NAPLES

Cafés

Naples is in love with European café culture. There are quite simply hundreds of excellent small cafés, from the traditional to the trendy, where you can have a great coffee and a pastry or two. Below are just a few of the recommended establishments.

Bar Mexico

Piazza Dante 86. Tel: 081 549 9330. Open: Mon–Sat 7am–8.30pm.

Caffè dell'Epoca

Via Costantinopoli 82. Tel: 081 291 722. Open: Mon–Sat 8am–8pm.

La Caffettiera

Piazza dei Martiri 30. Tel: 081 764 4243; www.lacaffettieraonline.com. Open: Mon–Fri 8am–7.30pm, Sat, Sun 7.30am–11pm.

Gambrinus

Via Chiaia 1–2. Tel: 081 417 582; www.caffegambrinus.com. Open: daily 7am–1am.

Restaurants

Gorizia ★

Located in one of Naples' favourite shopping areas in Vomero, this is a great spot for Neapolitan ladies who lunch. Pizza and hearty portions of pasta are served with aplomb.

Via Bernini 31. Tel: 081 578 2248. Open: Tue–Sun.

Hosteria Toledo ★

This simple eatery is a favourite with locals due to its ample servings and delicious takes on local favourites. While it boasts great views, the flavours are what you will remember most.

Via Giardinetto 78A. Tel: 081 421 257; www.hosteriatoledo.it. Open: noon–3pm Wed–Mon.

Leon d'Oro ★

This is a great place for fish dishes and pizza. Start with some typical Neapolitan antipasti, such as *zeppole* – basically fried pizza dough – and mini potato croquettes before tucking into generous portions of seafood pasta all washed

down with a bottle of dry white wine.
Piazza Dante 48. Tel: 081 549 9404. Open: Mon–Sat.

Osteria da Tonino ★
The busiest *osteria* in town, thanks to the antics of the husband-and-wife team who run the joint. Food is tasty and filling, if a little basic.
Via Santa Teresa a Chiaia 47. Tel: 081 421 533. Open: Mon–Fri 12.30–4pm, 7pm–1am. Closed: 2 weeks in Aug.

Pizzeria La Notizia ★
(*See p171 for details.*)

Sorbillo ★
(*See p171 for details.*)

Un Sorriso Integrale ★
Tucked away behind Piazza Bellini, this vegetarian restaurant is well worth the search. The menu includes macrobiotic options and fabulous organic Falanghina (local white wine), the atmosphere is relaxed and friendly and the prices surprisingly low.
Vico San Pietro a Maiella 6, Piazza Bellini. Tel: 081 455 026; www.sorrisointegrale.com Open: Mon–Sat.

Amici Miei ★★
Enjoy a change of pace at this restaurant that specialises in meat! You won't find seafood anywhere on the menu here, just rich steaks, drumsticks and pasta with meaty sauces.
Via Monte di Dio 77. Tel: 081 764 6063; www.ristoranteamicimiei.com. Open: Tue–Sun noon–3.30pm. Closed: Jul, Aug.

Cantina della Sapienza ★★
The best Neapolitan home cooking in the city (if you don't get an invite into a private home, that is). Order any of the traditional dishes and you won't go far wrong.
Via della Sapienza 40. Tel: 081 459 078. Open: Mon–Sat noon–3.30pm. Closed: Aug.

La Stanza del Gusto ★★
This amazing establishment is on three floors: the basement has

Café culture, Amalfi

deli delights and fine wines, the ground floor is a bar-*osteria* and the top floor has a smart restaurant serving dishes made from predominantly organic produce.
Via Costantinopoli 100. Open: Mon eve–Sat. Tel: 081 401 578; www.lastanzadelgusto.com

La Cantinella ★★★
A temple of food. Elaborate fish dishes are the most noteworthy items on the menu.
Via Nazario Sauro 23. Tel: 081 764 8684; www.lacantinella.it. Open: Mon–Sat 12.30–3pm, 7.30–11.30pm. Closed: 2 weeks in Aug.

Ciro a Santa Brigida ★★★
Founded in 1932, this traditional, family-run eatery offers Neapolitan comfort food in a formal yet non-stuffy atmosphere.
Via Santa Brigida 71. Tel: 081 552 4072.

D'Angelo ★★★★
This distinguished restaurant has fed many famous diners, including Naples' own Sofia Loren. Not only is the food divine, the panorama is pretty heavenly too.
Via Aniello Falcone 203. Open: Wed–Sun. Tel: 081 578 9772; www.ristorantedangelo.com

AMALFI

Da Gemma ★★
A historic and popular venue specialising in good local cuisine. Try the *melanzane in salse di cioccolato* (aubergines in chocolate sauce) for a truly inspiring end to a fabulous meal.
Via Fra' Gerardo Sasso 10. Tel: 089 871 345; www.trattoriadagemma.com. Open: Thur–Tue 12.30–2.45pm, 8–11pm.

'A Paranza ★★★★
Exquisite seafood dishes. The octopus comes highly recommended. Go for the house white wine, produced just down the street in Ravello.
Traversa Dragone 2. Tel: 089 871 840. Open: Jul–mid-Sept daily 12.30–3pm, 7.30pm–midnight; late Sept–Jun Mon, Wed–Sun 12.30–3pm, 7.30pm–midnight. Closed: 3 weeks in Dec.

La Caravella ★★★★
Amalfi's best restaurant, offering incredible seafood and an extensive wine list. The chefs pull out all the stops to make a meal here an experience you'll remember for a lifetime.
Via Matteo Camera 12. Tel: 089 871 029; www.ristorantelacaravella.it. Open: mid-Feb–early Nov, early Dec–early Jan Wed–Mon noon–2.30pm, 7.30–11pm.

CAPRI

La Capannina ★
The most consistently good restaurant in Capri. Come for by-the-book renditions of Capri specialities.
Via Le Botteghe 14. Tel: 081 837 0732; www.capannina-capri.com. Open: mid-Mar–Oct daily noon–3pm, 7.30pm–midnight; early Nov Mon, Tue, Thur–Sun noon–3pm, 7.30–11.30pm.

La Savardina da Edoardo ★
Game and pasta dishes galore at this converted farmhouse/restaurant. Makes a nice change from the usual fish.
Via Lo Capo 8. Tel: 081 837 6300. Open:

Jul, Aug daily noon–3pm, 7–11pm; mid-Mar–Jun, Sept, Oct Wed–Mon noon–3pm, 7–11pm.

Da Gemma ★★
A Capri institution. Good, reliable food. Author Graham Greene once called this place his home away from home. *Via Madre Serafina 6. Tel: 081 837 0461. Open: Aug daily noon–3pm, 7pm–midnight; Sept–Jul Tue–Sun noon–3pm, 7pm–midnight.*

Rondinella ★★
Capri can be quite a scene when you go out to eat. If you just want a tasty pizza and a bit of relaxed privacy, then this pizza parlour will do the trick. *Via G Orlandi 245, Anacapri. Tel: 081 837 1223. Open: daily noon–3pm, 7–11pm. Closed: Jul–mid-Sept Thur; Nov–Easter.*

Il Riccio ★★★
Just minutes away from the Grotta Azzurra, it's no surprise that the décor is distinctly blue. Part of the Capri Palace Hotel, this is the place to come for seafood, including a buffet of raw fish, fresh from the water to your terrace.
Via Grazola 4, località Grotta Azzurra.
Tel: 081 837 1380.
Closed: Nov–Mar.

ISCHIA

Trattoria il Focolare ★
Tradition with a twist is what's on offer at this romantic restaurant boasting a menu packed with old favourites and creative alternatives.
Via Cretajo al Croscefisso 3, Barano d'Ischia.
Tel: 081 902 944; www.trattoriailfocolare.it.
Open: Aug daily 12.30–3pm, 7.30–11.30pm; Sept–Oct, Dec–Jul Mon, Tue, Thur, Fri 7.30–11.30pm, Sat, Sun 12.30–3pm, 7.30–11.30pm.
Closed: Nov.

Il Faro ★★
This restaurant is a no-frills establishment, but concentrates on the food – superb seafood from the humble anchovy to calamari and lobster. If you book in advance you can savour the specialities: fish soup and Ischian rabbit.

The best local produce

Spiaggia di Maroni, Barano d'Ischia. Tel: 081 990 052. Closed: Nov–Easter.

La Romantica ★★★

This fish-focused tourist-friendly eatery has hosted some notorious big names, including Josephine Baker. On sunny days, choose a table on the terrace overlooking the old port.

Via Marina 46. Tel: 081 997 345. Open: daily noon–3pm, 7pm–midnight. Closed: Nov–Mar Wed.

O Purticciuli ★★★★

Family-friendly establishment located right on the harbour of Ischia Ponte. The seafood dishes are especially fresh and delicious.

Rive Droite 42, Ischia Porto. Tel: 081 993 222. Open: daily 12.30–3pm, 7.30–11pm.

Positano

Il Capitano ★

Positano's finest eatery cooks up a wealth of local dishes. Competent and classic is the name of the game.

Via Pasitea 119. Tel: 089 875 010; www.hotelmontemare.it. Open: daily noon–3pm, 7.30–10.30pm. Closed: Nov–Mar.

'O Guarracino ★

Location, location, location is what makes this restaurant so special. Enjoy the scenic veranda near the breathtaking cliffs overlooking Fornillo beach.

Via Positanesi d'America 12. Tel: 089 875 794; www.loguarracino.net. Open: daily 12.30–3pm, 7pm–midnight. Closed: Nov–Easter.

Il Ritrovo ★

A rustic restaurant boasting a fine wooden terrace with views down the valley to the sea. The vegetable antipasti are excellent.

Via Montepertuso 77. Tel: 089 812 005; www.ilritrovo.com. Open: May–Oct daily 12.30–3pm, 7pm–midnight; Feb–Apr, Nov, Dec Thur–Tue 12.30–3pm, 7pm–midnight. Closed: Jan, 1 week in Feb.

Procida

Caracale ★★★

Seafood is the speciality of this pretty eatery that also has meat and veggie dishes on the menu.

Via Marina Corricella 62. Tel: 081 896 9192. Open: noon–3pm, 7–11pm.

La Conchiglia ★★★

An incredibly romantic, family-run eatery on Chiaia beach. A boat ride is necessary to take

YOUR FRIENDLY, NEIGHBOURHOOD *ACQUAFRESCAI*

In the days when a drink of Neapolitan water could lead to something more than your thirst being quenched, a distinctly local business was developed to help soothe the stomachs of Campania's anxious residents. *Acquafrescai* (fresh-water sellers) may no longer be required now that the threat of cholera has dwindled, but the tradition lives on. On hot summer days, stallholders sell gallons of their natural drinks. Especially loved is the fizzing *spremuta di limone*, a cocktail of fresh lemons, carbonated spring water and bicarbonate of soda. For a true Neapolitan experience, head over to the brass counter in Piazza Teodoro Monticelli and gulp your way to contentedness.

you to the intimate tables. And the food is certainly no let-down. Dig in to incredible antipasti, pasta, local fish and fresh veggies.
Access from steps at Via Pizzaco, Discesa Graziella. Tel: 081 896 7602; www.laconchigliaristorante.com. Open: daily 12.30–3pm, 7.30–11pm. Closed: mid-Nov–Mar.

Sorrento

Mondo Bio ★
Sorrento's only vegetarian restaurant is a delightful tonic for green eaters or those just looking for something other than meat-feast pizza during their stay.
Via degli Aranci 146–148. Tel: 081 807 5694. Open: Mon–Sat 8.30am–8.30pm. Also offers take-away service.

Pizzeria Aurora ★
Massive variety of award-winning oven-fired pizzas. Great lunch stop, with something for everyone.
Piazza Tasso 10. Tel: 081 878 1248; www.pizzeriaaurora.com. Open: daily noon–4pm, 6.30pm–midnight. Closed: Mon in winter. Phone to check opening.

Ristorante Vittoria ★
The ultimate Grand Tour dining experience. White-jacketed waiters and silver service. It's all here and more.
Grand Hotel Excelsior, Piazza Tasso 34. Tel: 081 807 1044; www.exvitt.it. Open: daily 1–2.15pm, 7.45–10.30pm.

Zi'Ntonio ★★
This friendly seafood and pizza restaurant on the marina is an attractive option for a break and great value.
Via Marina Grande 180. Tel: 081 807 3033; www.zintoniomare.it. Open: daily noon–3pm, 7–11pm.

Il Buco ★★★
Situated in the converted cellars of an old convent, Il Buco dishes up *nouvelle* Italian cuisine. Portions look small but are surprisingly filling and impeccably presented.
Rampa Marina Piccola 5. Tel: 081 878 2354; www.ilbucoristorante.it. Open: daily noon–3.30pm, 7–11.30pm.

Canonico ★★★
It isn't exactly a must-do, but this restaurant specialising in Sorrentine favourites offers consistent service and a great location.
Piazza Tasso 5. Tel: 081 878 3277. Open: Tue–Sun noon–3.30pm, 7–11.30pm.

Fruit and spices shop, Via dei Tribunali, Naples

The dawn of the pizza

The chefs of Naples claim that this delicious delicacy, now ubiquitous throughout the world, was born in the wood-fired ovens of this very city. As such, the status of the dish has been elevated to an art form. Locals will cling to their favourite *pizzerie* with a passion almost as strong as their support for the local football team.

Once a meal for only the poorest of the city, the Neapolitan pizza is now enjoyed by all. In this city you will only find one kind of crust available: thin, crisp and dry, unlike the thick, doughy types found in US cities.

Many of Naples' best *pizze* are made in rustic locations where staff speak not a word of English and have never heard of a reservation. Don't even think about ordering pineapple on your pizza in a place like this. It will probably cause many a jaw to drop and a lot of derisive laughing. Don't be put off by queues: these places turn over their customers at a remarkably fast rate. To place your order, make your presence known to the head waiter or you may be standing there all night. You can ask for just about any combination of pizza toppings you like, but most locals opt for the *margherita*.

Traditional pizzas include:

Caprese: Fresh cherry tomatoes and mozzarella. A few leaves of *rucola* or *rughetta* (rocket) are optional.

Capricciosa: Tomato, black olives, artichokes and ham.

Margherita: Tomato, mozzarella, basil and oil.

Marinara: Tomato, oregano, garlic and oil.

Prosciutto crudo e rucola in bianco: Parma ham, mozzarella and fresh rocket.

Ripieno: A pizza folded pastry-style, stuffed with mozzarella, ricotta and salami and topped with tomato and basil.

Ripieno fritto: A deep-fried version of the above, often containing pieces of pig fat in the filling.

Salsiccia e friarielli: Mozzarella, sausage and *friarielli* (a form of local spinach).

Some of the better *pizzerie* to try out include:

Antonio e Antonio

Over 40 different types of pizza are produced at this eatery staffed by chefs who trained at some of Naples' finest restaurants.

Via Partenope 26. Tel: 081 245 1987;

www.antonioeantonio.net. Open: daily 12.30–3.30pm, 7.30–11.30pm.

Brandi

The place that claims to have invented the *margherita*. Ex-US President Bill Clinton is a former patron.

Salita Sant'Anna di Palazzo 1. Tel: 081 416 928; www.brandi.it. Open: daily 12.30–3.30pm, 7pm–midnight. Closed: 1 week in Aug.

Da Michele

Minimalist eatery offering only two types of pizza, made perfectly: the *margherita* and *marinara*.

Via Sersale 1. Tel: 081 553 9204; www.damichele.net. Open: May–Dec daily 10am–11pm; Jan–Apr Mon–Sat 10am–11pm. Closed: 2 weeks in Aug.

Di Matteo

High on function and low on form, the pizzas are superb. The décor, however, leaves a lot to be desired.

Via dei Tribunali 94. Tel: 081 455 262. Open: Mon–Sat 9am–midnight. Closed: 2 weeks in Aug.

Ettore

Varied menu of pizzas and other simple dishes. Uniquely, the speciality of the house is their *calzoni* – pizzas folded and stuffed with traditional topping ingredients.

Via Santa Lucia 56. Tel: 081 764 0498. Open: Tue–Sun 12.30–3.30pm, 7.30–11.30pm.

Pizzeria La Notizia

Another pizzeria along spartan lines so beloved of Neapolitans. *Pizzaiolo* Enzo Coccia creates the fine pizzas served here.

Via Caravaggio 53–55. Tel: 081 714 2155. Open: Tue–Sun, evenings only.

Sorbillo

The oldest and the best of the Sorbillo *pizzerie*. What it lacks in refinement, it makes up for in sublime pizzas, friendly service and a minuscule bill. Not to be missed.

Via dei Tribunali 35. Tel: 339 191 2760. Open: Mon–Sat.

Naples, home of the pizza

Accommodation

The Italian State Tourist Board operates their own star classification system for hotels. The most luxurious is classified as a five-star, while a comfortable, simple pensione *is classified as a one-star. There are no five-star properties in the city of Naples, even though its four-star hotels are often jaw-droppingly luxurious.*

During high season from June to September, at Christmas and New Year, hotels are often booked months, if not years, in advance – especially on weekends. This is especially the case for properties in Capri, Ischia and along the Amalfi Coast. Another busy time is during the period of *Maggio dei Monumenti*, when visitors flock to the city to visit churches, historical sites and private chapels that are usually closed to the general public and local hotel owners raise their prices accordingly.

If you're on a budget, Naples has plenty of options to choose from. Most low-cost hotels stick close to the decidedly unsavoury Piazza Garibaldi. Standards vary widely, so be sure to check your room before you sign on the dotted line. In Capri, Ischia, Procida and along the Amalfi Coast, budget options are decidedly thin on the ground. Prices usually start at about €100 for a single bed per night and go up, up and away. Surprisingly, even these outrageously priced properties fill well in advance during high season. Book ahead if you are planning an overnight stay.

If you decide to use the services of a hotel booking agency, be advised that there are no services on offer through any government-sponsored tourist boards. All booking agencies are privately owned and profit-minded, and you will most certainly pay for the ease and convenience.

For a list of each area's hotels, try contacting the local **Associazione Albergatori** (Hoteliers' Association) through their website *www.campaniahotels.com*. Otherwise, if you find yourself stranded at the airport with no bed for the night, give **Prom Hotels** (*Airport location. Tel: 081 789 6716; Fax 081 789 6717*) a whirl. A second location at Stazione Centrale is available if you arrive in town by train. Alternatively, just contact any of the hotels listed below directly.

Price per room, per night

★	under €60
★★	€60–€120
★★★	€120–€180
★★★★	€180–€240
★★★★★	over €240

NAPLES

Luxury hotels

Hotel Palazzo Turchini ★★★
Can't remember where the hotel is? Look for the Fountain of Neptune and you're home. A stone's throw from many of the major sights, it has a lovely terrace with city views.
Via Medina 21.
Tel: 081 551 0606;
www.palazzoturchini.it

Mediterraneo ★★★
A great place to set off on your tours of the city and easy to reach from the airport. A modern hotel in a neoclassical building with a panoramic terrace overlooking the Bay of Naples.
Via Nuova Ponte di Tappia 25.
Tel: 081 797 0001; www.mediterraneonapoli.com

Palazzo Albardieri ★★★
Set in the heart of Royal Naples, this is a smart hotel ideal for exploring the sites and the waterfront.
Via Albardieri 38.
Tel: 081 415 278;
www.palazzoalabardieri.it

Excelsior ★★★★
Luxurious accommodation on the waterfront, with rooms overlooking Vesuvius and Castel dell'Ovo. Old-style elegance and a terrace with views to die for.
Via Partenope 48.
Tel: 081 764 0111;
www.excelsior.it

Hotel Una ★★★★
Situated in the lively Piazza Garibaldi, this modern hotel is part of a chain. The cocktail bar has excellent views over the heart of the city and there is a hotel library.
Piazza Garibaldi 9/10.
Tel: 081 563 6901;
www.unahotels.it

Palazzo Decumani ★★★★
A super-swish hotel in the historic heart of the city, you are just minutes away from the Duomo. The rooms are airy, elegant and large.
Piazzetta Giustino Fortunato 8.
Tel: 081 410 9144; www.palazzodecumani.com

Santa Lucia ★★★★
Situated on the waterfront and close to the castles and Piazza del Plebiscito, Hotel Santa Lucia is swish, stylish and exuding charm. A great place to come for a city break.
Via Partenope 46.
Tel: 081 764 0666.

Grand Hotel Parker's ★★★★★
One of the most famous hotels in Naples, and it's not hard to see why: luxury surroundings, breathtaking views, prompt service.
Corso Vittorio Emanuele 135. Tel: 081 761 2474;
www.grandhotelparkers.com

Budget hotels

Some of the more affordable hotels are:

Art Resort Galleria Umberto I ★★
This has to be one of the most unusual locations in town. Set inside the famous Galleria Umberto I, the hotel is decorated in neoclassical style and has great vistas of the gallery from its interior.
Galleria Umberto I 83.

Tel: 081 497 6281; www.artresortgalleriaumberto.it

Ausonia ★★

To say that this hotel has a nautical feel does not do the expression justice. Overlooking Porto Mergellina, prepare to brace the mainsail in this friendly family-run establishment.

Via Caracciolo 11. Tel: 081 682 278; www.hotelausonianapoli.com

B & B Bellini ★★

Pristine and comfortable B&B in the leafy Piazza Bellini.

Piazza Bellini 68. Tel: 081 060 7338; www.bbbellini.it

Cappella Vecchia 11 ★★

Situated in Royal Naples, this bright and clean B&B is an ideal spot for those travelling to the islands.

Vicolo Santa Maria a Cappella Vecchia 11. Tel: 081 240 5117; www.cappellavecchia11.it

Donna Regina B&B ★★

If you like contemporary art, then this is the place for you: an attractive home just steps away from MADRe, Naples' modern art museum.

Via Luigi Settembrini 80. Tel: 081 446 799; www.discovernaples.net

Hotel Piazza Bellini ★★

Though housed in a 16th-century palace, this contemporary and colourful hotel will bring you back to the 21st century. Set in the heart of the Centro Storico, it's a great place for sightseeing and has excellent eateries just around the corner.

Via Costantinopoli 101. Tel: 081 451 732; www.hotelpiazzabellini.com

Hotel Villa Ranieri ★★

This hotel in the Sanità neighbourhood has an old-fashioned elegance and with only 14 rooms retains the feel of a private residence. If the weather is good, you can enjoy your breakfast in the splendid hotel garden.

Corso Amadeo di Savoia 29. Tel: 081 741 6308; www.hotelvillaranieri.com

Chiaja Hotel de Charme ★★★

This comfortable and friendly hotel has an old-fashioned feel to it. The rooms are all individually furnished and even have names. A great starting point for sightseeing.

Via Chiaia 216. Tel: 081 415 555; www.hotelchiaja.it

Hostels

Surprisingly, hostels aren't really a popular option in the area. Two options to consider are:

Agriturismo Il Casolare di Tobia ★

A great place to come if you are travelling alone. Friendly and with evening events, this gives both rural calm and handy access to Naples.

Contrada Coste Fondi di Baia, Via Pietro Fabris 12, Bacoli. Tel: 081 523 5193; www.datobia.it. Please note that this hostel is located in a farmhouse outside of the city centre.

Ostello Mergellina (Youth Hostel) ★

A bargain for those travelling on a budget. Close to the ports on the waterfront and a short bus ride from the centre.

Salita della Grotta a Piedigrotta 23. Tel: 081 761 2346; www.hihostels.com

Private homes

Try the following service if you prefer to rent an apartment or just a room in a private home.

Discover Naples ★★

Offering a range of B&Bs, this friendly agency also has some good-value apartments in both Naples and Capri.

Via Luigi Settembrini 80.
Tel: 081 446 799;
www.discovernaples.net

Rent a Bed ★

If you wait until the last minute, you can pick up some great offers both in Naples and on the surrounding Amalfi Coast.

Vico San Carlo alle Mortelle 14.
Tel: 081 417 721;
www.rentabed.com

Camping

Two registered campsites are located in nearby Pozzuoli, but neither is within easy reach of the city centre. Both are situated in rustic beauty spots.

Averno ★

This attractive campsite also has bungalows to rent. Restaurants and a disco are here so you don't need to travel for your entertainment.

Via Montenuovo Licola Patria 85, Arco Felice Lucrino, Pozzuoli.
Tel: 081 804 2666;
www.averno.it

Vulcano Solfatara ★

Located within a natural park and named after the nearby volcano, this site also has a pool, mini-market and sports facilities.

Via Solfatara 161, Pozzuoli.
Tel: 081 526 2341;
www.solfatara.it

AMALFI

Elegant hotels make up the bulk of what's on offer, including two converted from monasteries.

Hotel Lidomare ★★

Situated near Piazza del Duomo, this building dates back to the 1300s. The hotel is clean and bright, with a terrace overlooking the coast.

Largo Duchi Piccolomini 9.
Tel: 089 871 332;
www.lidomare.it

Hotel Amalfi ★★★

Just off Piazza del Duomo, this is a bargain hotel. The rooms are clean and all have pretty majolica floor tiles. In the summer months, enjoy your breakfast on the roof terrace.

Via dei Pastai 3.
Tel: 089 872 440;
www.hamalfi.it
Closed: 5 Jan–Mar.

Santa Caterina ★★★★★

This beautiful villa has won numerous awards and deservedly so. Great pool, jaw-dropping vistas over the sea and honeymoon suites boasting their own infinity pool, this hotel ticks all the right boxes.

Via Mauro Comite.
Tel: 089 871 012;
www.hotelsantacaterina.it

CAPRI

Prepare to take out a second mortgage if you are looking to stay on Capri in high season. Prices are deliberately inflated in order to encourage a higher class of tourist. Many hotels close from November to mid-March, with limited opening during the Christmas period. Book in advance to avoid disappointment.

La Tosca ★★

This small and friendly hotel has just ten rooms,

all of them airy and pretty, most of them with panoramic views. The Charterhouse of San Giacomo and other Capri sights are a short walk away.
Via Birago 5.
Tel: 081 837 0989;
www.latoscahotel.com.
Closed: Nov–Mar.

Hotel Villa Traiano ★★★
This Liberty-style villa has recently been restored. The rooftop terrace and pretty courtyard are great spots for relaxing after a hard day on the beach.
Viale Dei Rettori 9.
Tel: 0824 326 241;
www.hotelvillatraiano.it.
Closed: 2 weeks Aug.

La Reginella ★★★
A hillside hotel offering spectacular views of the sea and surrounding park area, this is a moderately priced option for visitors to Capri.
Via Matermania 36.
Tel: 081 837 0500;
www.hotellareginella.com.
Closed: Nov–Easter.

Villa Carmencita ★★★
This simple hotel with a small pool is conveniently situated in the centre of town. The staff are friendly and it's a good place for families.
Viale T De Tommaso.
Tel: 081 837 1360;
www.carmencitacapri.com.
Closed: Nov–Mar.

Villa Krupp ★★★
Though not the most sumptuous of hotels on the island, Villa Krupp provides friendly service in relaxing surroundings. The vistas are exceptional and its lofty location means it is on the route of various walking itineraries.
Via G Matteotti 12.
Tel: 081 837 0362;
www.villakrupp.it.
Closed: Nov–Mar.

La Minerva ★★★★
A peaceful retreat overlooking the sea. All the deluxe and superior rooms have coastal views, as do the attractive gardens and pool.
Via Occhio Marino 8.
Tel: 081 837 0374;
www.laminervacapri.com.
Closed: Nov–Feb.

Capri Palace ★★★★★
This is, quite possibly, the most fabulous hotel on an island swarming with fabulous hotels. An award-winning spa, an art gallery exhibiting famous works and practically perfect service all add up to an unforgettable experience.
Via Capodimonte 2B.
Tel: 081 978 0111;
www.capripalace.com.
Closed: Nov–Easter.

ISCHIA

Ischia rivals Capri in hotel quality and price. Once again, high season is busy and beds are like gold dust. Book ahead.

Il Vitigno ★
A great place for nature lovers, this converted villa is located in Forio in the midst of vineyards. The rustic rooms are simply furnished and there's a small pool.
Via Bocca 31.
Tel: 081 998 307;
www.ilvitigno.com.
Closed: Sept–Easter.

Hotel La Marticana ★★
This hotel perhaps offers the best value for money on the island. The rooms are clean and simply furnished and the hotel sits in lush gardens.
Via Quercia 48.
Tel: 081 993 230;
www.lamarticana.it

Il Monastero ★★
Beautifully converted monastery close to the

Castello Aragonese. Many of the ingredients on the menu come from the hotel's organic vegetable garden.
Via Pontile Aragonese.
Tel: 081 992 435;
www.albergoilmonastero.it.
Closed: Nov–Easter.

Casa Apollon ★★★★
Next door to the more sumptuous Miramare Hotel, the hotel is set in the vast grounds of its more glamorous sister. Guests have free use of the twelve pools and fitness programmes at the nearby Aphrodite-Apollon spa.
Via Maddalena 29.
Tel: 081 999 219;
www.hotelmiramare.it.
Closed: Nov–Mar.

Hotel Casa Celestino ★★★★
With just 20 rooms, all with a sea view, this is a relaxed and friendly hotel. The hotel terrace juts out over the sea, offering a superb panorama.
Via Chiaia di Rose 20.
Tel: 081 999 213;
www.casacelestino.it.
Closed: Nov–Mar.

Park Hotel Miramare ★★★★★
Possibly one of the friendliest hotels on the island, it has all the amenities to make your stay a pleasure, including excellent spa treatments.
Via Comandante Maddalena 29.
Tel: 081 999 219;
www.hotelmiramare.it.
Closed: end Oct–Easter.

POSITANO

Positano has plenty of hotels to choose from, with many built for function rather than form. Converted villas and 18th-century residences, while expensive, are your best bet.

Maria Luisa ★
Claiming to be the cheapest hotel in Positano, the *pensione* is situated in a pedestrian zone, just minutes away from the beach. Most of the rooms have balconies with panoramic views.
Via Fornillo 42.
Tel: 089 875 023; www.pensionemarialuisa.com.
Closed: Nov–Mar.

California Residence ★★★
All of the rooms here have views either of the old town or of the sea. Simply furnished and airy, this is a welcoming hotel in a great location.
Via Cristoforo Colombo 141.
Tel: 089 875 382; www.hotelcaliforniapositano.com

Villa Franca ★★★★
With a rooftop pool, a wellness centre where you can slip into a sauna or have a massage, and a bar and terrace with views of the old town and the coast, this is one of the best hotels in town.
Viale Pasitea 318.
Tel: 089 875 655;
www.villafrancahotel.it

San Pietro ★★★★★
Celebrating its 40th birthday in 2010, this charming hotel combines informal elegance with top-class service. The private beach is situated in a hidden cove.
Via Laurito 2.
Tel: 089 875 455;
www.ilsanpietro.it.
Closed: end Oct–Mar.

PROCIDA

Procida's best bets are family-run *pensiones* in the fishermen's quarter.

Hotel Celeste ★
Inspired by the azure sky and sea, this hotel takes

blue as its theme in the décor and furnishings. Close to the marina, it's a good spot from which to head off on outings.
Via Rivoli 6.
Tel: 081 896 7488;
www.hotelceleste.it

Casa Sul Mare ★★
Casa Sul Mare is an intimate hotel with just ten rooms – all with a sea view – guaranteeing excellent service. Boat rides and scuba diving are offered at discounted prices.
Salita Castello 13.
Tel: 081 896 8799;
www.lacasasulmare.it.
Closed: Jan, Feb.

Hotel Savoia ★★
This is the oldest hotel on the island and boasts a swimming pool, restaurant and lemon groves. Inspired by the lovely garden, each room is named after a flower.
Via Lavadera 32.
Tel: 081 896 7616;
www.procida.net/savoia

Solcalante ★★★
Perched on the cliffs and offering great views of the sea, the little hotel is surrounded by greenery. Relax in a hotel hammock after a walk to the nearby beach.
Via Serra 1.
Tel: 081 810 1856;
www.solcalante.it

RAVELLO

Ravello has a number of charming hotels, all with colourful histories.

Hotel Parsifal ★★★
An ex-convent dating back to the 13th century, this is one of the few budget hotels in Ravello and one of the best. Nineteen rooms surround the cloister and the restaurant terrace provides stunning views across the sea.
Viale G d'Anna 5.
Tel: 089 857 144;
www.hotelparsifal.com

Hotel Villa Maria ★★★★
An oasis of peace, Villa Maria has spectacular views of the Dragone valley and the sea. Guests can use nearby sister establishment Hotel Giordano's pool.
Via Santa Chiara 2.
Tel: 089 857 255;
www.villamaria.it

Caruso Belvedere ★★★★★
A remarkable hotel situated at the highest point of Ravello. The infinity pool seems to stretch out into the sea below. A wonderful wellness centre and breathtaking terrace restaurant make this a truly magnificent establishment.
Piazza San Giovanni del Toro 2. Tel: 089 858 801;
www.hotelcaruso.com.
Closed: winter (variable).

Hotel Rufolo ★★★★★
Once one of the most important private family homes in Ravello, this attractively converted villa not only has great rooms and a wellness centre, it boasts perhaps the loveliest gardens in town.
Via San Francesco 1.
Tel: 089 857 133;
www.hotelrufolo.it.
Closed: Jan, Feb.

Palumbo ★★★★★
Yet another medieval residence-cum-hotel, the Palumbo's architecture is a wonderful mishmash of different periods. The rooms are large and overlook the stunning coastline. Dining in the frescoed dining room with paintings by one of Caravaggio's pupils.
Via S Giovanni del Toro 16.
Tel: 089 857 244;
www.hotelpalumbo.it

Rossellini's Palazzo Sasso ★★★★★
Palazzo Sasso was once a 12th-century family villa and is rated as one of the world's finest hotels. Boasting a restaurant with two Michelin stars, a sumptuous wellness centre and jaw-dropping coastal views from luxurious suites, this hotel deserves the many international awards it has won.
Via San Giovanni del Toro 28.
Tel: 089 818 181; www.palazzosasso.com

Villa Cimbrone ★★★★★
This marvellous villa is set among vast verdant gardens and many visitors flock here to see them and admire the views from the belvedere. D H Lawrence and Churchill are just two of the many erstwhile guests who have graced this gracious hotel.
Via Santa Chiara 26.
Tel: 089 857 459; www.villacimbrone.com.
Closed: Nov–Mar.

SORRENTO

Hotel Mignon Meublé ★
This petite and pretty hotel provides friendly and affordable accommodation in the heart of Sorrento. All rooms are air-conditioned.
Via Sersale 9.
Tel: 081 807 3824; www.sorrentohotelmignon.com

Hotel Gardenia ★★
The hotel is in the heart of Sorrento, just a short stroll from the historic centre. There's a pool, tennis court and pretty garden.
Corso Italia 258.
Tel: 081 877 2365; www.hotelgardenia.com

Parco dei Principi ★★★★
Built on a cliff edge with stunning views overlooking the sea, this high-class establishment was designed by one of Italy's most famous modern architects, Giò Ponti. It has a pool, private beach and excellent wellness centre.
Via Rota 1, Sant'Agnello.
Tel: 081 878 4644; www.grandhotelparcodeiprincipi.net

Bellevue Syrene ★★★★★
Set on the steep coastline, this hotel has sweeping views of the bay of Naples, with Mount Vesuvius towering in the background. The décor is a successful mix of the classical and the modern, a great example of this being the suite Roccia carved out of a Roman grotto. Amazing.
Piazza Bella Vittoria 5.
Tel: 081 878 1024; www.bellevue.it.
Closed: Jan, Feb.

Excelsior Vittoria ★★★★★
Choose from quiet rooms amid the idyllic gardens or vast suites with sweeping terraces overlooking the sea. A hotel since 1834, you can experience the luxury previously enjoyed by kings, artists and celebrities.
Piazza Tasso 34.
Tel: 081 877 7111; www.exvitt.it

Grand Hotel Cocumella ★★★★★
A luxury hotel offering some of the finest views of the Sorrento coast from its lush gardens and panoramic terraces. Its restaurants are particularly fine.
Via Cocumella 7.
Tel: 081 878 2933; www.cocumella.com.
Closed: Nov–Mar.

Practical guide

Arriving

Formalities

Visitors to Italy who are citizens of the UK, Ireland, Australia, the USA, Canada or New Zealand will need a passport, but not a visa, for stays of up to three months. After that time, they must apply for a *permesso di soggiorno* (permit to stay). If you are travelling from other countries, you may need a visa, and it is best to check before you leave home.

By air

Capodichino Airport (*Tel: call centre from Italy: 848 888 777; from abroad: 081 751 5471; www.gesac.it*) is southern Italy's largest international airport and it is about 8km (5 miles) from the Stazione Centrale rail station. There are a number of ways to get from the airport into the centre of town.

Alibus: Connects to the Stazione Centrale and Piazza Municipio (near the ferry port) via blue buses departing from near the airport's arrivals lounge. *Tel: 800 639 525; www.anm.it. Departs every 20min. Operates 6am–midnight daily.*

To Sorrento and the Sorrento Peninsula: Autolinee Curreri (*Tel: 081 801 5420*) runs six buses daily from outside arrivals. Tickets: €6.

By public bus

Local orange bus number 3S runs from outside the arrivals lounge to Piazza Garibaldi and the ferry port. *Departs every 30min Mon–Fri 6.10am–9.30pm, Sat 7am–9.30pm.*

By taxi

A fare from the airport to central Naples should be about €20. There is a surcharge of €2.60 for all airport runs.

By rail

You are most likely to arrive at the Stazione Centrale in the heart of Naples on the Piazza Garibaldi. Some late-night long-distance rail services terminate at Stazione Campi Flegrei in the eastern suburbs.

By sea

The ports nearest to Naples are Molo Beverello, Mergellina and Pozzuoli.

Molo Beverello: Naples' premier ferry and hydrofoil port. Arrivals and departures to/from Capri, Ischia, Procida, Sorrento and the Amalfi Coast. Mediterranean cruise-liners also disembark from the city-centre dock.

Mergellina: Hydrofoil services to and from Capri, Ischia and Procida.

Pozzuoli: Car ferries for Procida and Ischia. The port is located 12km (7½ miles) northwest of Naples.

For details of up-to-date train and ferry services consult the *Thomas Cook European Rail Timetable*, available to buy online at *www.thomascookpublishing.com* or from Thomas Cook in the UK (*Tel: 01733 416477*).

Cars and driving

Breakdown

The **ACI** (*Tel: 803 116*) and **Touring Club Italia** (*Tel: 081 420 3485; www.touringclub.it*) offer breakdown services.

Car hire

Most car-hire companies will have offices at the airport. The majority of their cars will be manual, but there are a limited number of automatic cars for hire. To get the best deal and guarantee availability, book a car before you leave home. Booking on the internet can give considerable savings. To rent a car in Italy you must be over 21 (25 to rent a larger-cylinder car) and be able to produce a full valid driving licence from your country of residence. The usual hire rate quoted will cover third-party/liability insurance, unlimited mileage, VAT and passenger indemnity insurance. It is recommended that you take out the additional collision damage waiver, so that you are not liable for replacement of the car. If you have an accident or if the car breaks down, you should inform the car-hire company immediately.

Driving

Nothing can prepare you for the sheer volume of cars on the streets of the city. Avoid the rush-hour traffic, which is at its worst during wet weather and on Fridays. Don't drink and drive.

Fuel

There are few petrol stations in the centre of Naples. In every petrol station there are usually unleaded, leaded and diesel pumps. Credit card facilities are not always available.

Parking

Finding parking in Naples is virtually impossible. If you do find a space, you will need to purchase a pay-and-display ticket, scratch card or parking debit card from street-side dispensing machines, *tabacchi* or *edicole* (news-stands). Look for blue lines on the road to ensure that your space is permitted. The streets are patrolled by traffic wardens who issue tickets liberally for transgressors. Illegal parking attendants operate in many areas: they will claim to 'look after' your car for about €1. The safest option is to use a pay car park, especially if you need to leave your car overnight and/or have foreign registration. If you do park illegally, your car will be clamped and/or you will pay a fine, or it might be towed away and you will have to pay to remove it from the pound.

In the event that you do find a space on the road that isn't marked with a blue line, go ahead and park – with three exceptions. Look for signs saying *passo carrabile* (access at all times), *sosta vietata* (no parking) and disabled parking spaces marked with yellow lines. The sign *zona rimozione* (tow-away area) means no parking and is valid until the end of the street, or until the next tow-away sign with a red line through it.

Via Brin (*Via B Brin. Tel: 081 763 2855*) runs an 850-car facility between the

Stazione Centrale and the port. Find it by taking the Porto exit from the ring road or motorway. Shuttle buses leave for the ferry port at Molo Beverello every ten minutes.

Traffic regulations

Drive on the right and use a seatbelt. Always carry your driving licence with you. The law states that you need to carry a hazard triangle in your car at all times, and remember the following tips to avoid an accident:

- Flashing your lights means that you will **not** slow down or give way.
- Locals often ignore red lights, so approach any junction with caution. If traffic lights flash amber, stop and give way to the right.
- Watch out for scooters and pedestrians. Both will fully expect you to stop if they decide to move in front of you.

For traffic updates, *Tel: 166 664 477* for 24-hour information with English-speaking operators. Cars are forbidden on the island of Capri.

Crime

Crime has always been a big problem for the city of Naples. Its reputation is actually far worse than the reality. Petty theft (bag-snatching, pickpocketing) is the most common form of trouble for tourists, and activity is particularly high in the much-frequented historic sites. You are unlikely to experience violence or assault, which occur mainly in the context of gangland activities.

Don't carry too much cash and avoid walking around alone very late at night on badly lit streets (especially if you are a woman). Your hotel will warn you about particular areas to avoid.

Attitude is everything. Look as if you know what you're doing and where you're going. Do not carry your wallet in your back pocket, especially on buses. Keep your bags closed with your hand on them at all times, and do not leave your bag or coat on the ground where you cannot see them. When walking down the street, be sure to wear camera straps and bags crossed over your chest. Make sure the bag and/or camera is on the side away from the street so as to prevent robberies from motorbike thieves. And whatever you do, stay away from cute children. Often, they are part of larger gangs and are masters at removing precious items.

Car theft is also a problem. Do not leave valuables in an unattended rental car (thieves can recognise the registration) or in a car with foreign registration.

Customs regulations

Duty-free goods are only available to those who visit Italy from outside the EU. You can also purchase duty-free goods if you are flying directly from Italy to a non-EU country, or if you fly to a non-EU country via an EU country stopover (but you must leave the EU on the same day). If you have come from outside the EU, you are allowed 200 cigarettes, 2 litres of wine and 1 litre of spirits. Particular emphasis is placed on the ban on importing foodstuffs, particularly meat products in the light of recent outbreaks of foot-and-mouth disease and BSE.

Electricity

The standard electrical current is 220 volts. Two-pin adaptor plugs can be purchased at most electrical shops.

Embassies and consulates

American Consulate Piazza della Repubblica, Mergellina. *Tel: 081 583 8111; http://naples.usconsulate.gov*

British Consulate Via dei Mille 40, Chiaia. *Tel: 081 423 8911; www.ukinitaly.fco.gov.uk*

Canadian Consulate Via G Carducci 29, Chiaia. *Tel: 081 401 338; www.international.gc.ca*

Australians and New Zealanders requiring diplomatic assistance should consult their embassies in Rome.

Emergency telephone numbers

The emergency telephone numbers in Italy are *113* and *112* (police), *115* (fire), *118* (ambulance), *803 116* (car breakdown), *1530* (coastguard) and *151* (forest rangers and mountain rescue).

Entertainment guides

The Naples Tourist Board produces a 'what's on' booklet, *Qui Napoli*, which lists cultural events, exhibitions and transport timetables. The national newspapers also provide listings of events – in Italian only.

Look out for *Le Pagine dell'Ozio* and *Leggo, City* and local newspaper

CONVERSION TABLE

FROM	TO	MULTIPLY BY
Inches	Centimetres	2.54
Feet	Metres	0.3048
Yards	Metres	0.9144
Miles	Kilometres	1.6090
Acres	Hectares	0.4047
Gallons	Litres	4.5460
Ounces	Grams	28.35
Pounds	Grams	453.6
Pounds	Kilograms	0.4536
Tons	Tonnes	1.0160

To convert back, for example from centimetres to inches, divide by the number in the third column.

MEN'S SUITS

UK	36	38	40	42	44	46	48
Rest of Europe	46	48	50	52	54	56	58
USA	36	38	40	42	44	46	48

DRESS SIZES

UK	8	10	12	14	16	18
France	36	38	40	42	44	46
Italy	38	40	42	44	46	48
Rest of Europe	34	36	38	40	42	44
USA	6	8	10	12	14	16

MEN'S SHIRTS

UK	14	14.5	15	15.5	16	16.5	17
Rest of Europe	36	37	38	39/40	41	42	43
USA	14	14.5	15	15.5	16	16.5	17

MEN'S SHOES

UK	7	7.5	8.5	9.5	10.5	11
Rest of Europe	41	42	43	44	45	46
USA	8	8.5	9.5	10.5	11.5	12

WOMEN'S SHOES

UK	4.5	5	5.5	6	6.5	7
Rest of Europe	38	38	39	39	40	41
USA	6	6.5	7	7.5	8	8.5

Il Mattino di Napoli for current arts and entertainment listings.

Health

Visitors from the EU are entitled to free treatment under the EU Reciprocal Medical Treatment Programme. The European Health Insurance Card is available free from *www.ehic.org.uk*, by phoning *0845 606 2030* or from post offices. If you need to see a doctor, tell the office that you want to be treated under EU social security arrangements. Visitors from countries outside the EU should ensure that they have adequate insurance cover before leaving. In an emergency, go to the *pronto soccorso* (casualty) department of one of the major hospitals.

In Naples:

Cardarelli (*Via Cardarelli 9. Tel: 081 747 1111*), Santobono (*Via M Fiore 6. Tel: 081 220 5111*).

On Capri:

Ospedale Capilupi (*Via Provinciale Anacapri. Tel: 081 838 1111*).

On Ischia:

Ospedale Anna Rizzoli (*Via Fundara 2. Tel: 081 507 9111*).

In Sorrento:

Ospedale Civico (*Corso Italia. Tel: 081 533 1111*).

The city council offers an interpreting service for emergency hospital treatment (*Tel: 081 533 5311/349 243 2403*).

Hiring a bicycle or scooter

Riding a bike is one of the best ways to see Naples, but be sure to wear a helmet at all times. If you need to hire a scooter, try one of the car rental agencies. For a bike try **Napoli Bike** (*Riviera di Chiaia 201. Tel: 081 411 934; www.napolibike.com*).

Insurance

You should take out personal travel insurance from your travel agent, tour operator or insurance company. It should give adequate cover for medical expenses, loss or theft, repatriation, personal liability, third-party motor insurance (but liability arising from motor accidents is not usually included) and cancellation expenses. If you hire a car, collision insurance (often called collision damage waiver or CDW) is usually compulsory and charged by the hirer, but it may be as much as 50 per cent of the hiring fee. Check with your own motor insurers before you leave, as you may already be covered for CDW on overseas hires.

Neither CDW nor your personal travel insurance will protect you from liability arising from an accident in a hire car. If you are likely to hire a car, you should obtain some extra cover. If you take your own motor vehicle on holiday, check with your motor insurers on your cover for damage, loss or theft of the vehicle and for liability. A Green Card (third-party cover) is recommended for those from European countries outside the EU.

Maps

The Osservatorio Turistico-Culturale on the Piazza del Plebiscito has probably the best selection of free maps of the city centre. When in other towns in the region, head to the local tourist office. News-stands, *tabacchi*, ports and tourist sites always have maps available for sale.

Media

English-language broadcasting is almost nonexistent, but most hotels will have satellite TV in the bedrooms.

Most Italian papers are strictly regional and very political. The largest daily in the city is *Il Mattino*; however, the Rome-based daily *La Repubblica* and Milan's *Corriere della Sera* both have Neapolitan sections. Sports coverage is extensive – especially when covering national football results. None of the above offer English-language sections. You can usually buy European versions of the British press and the *International Herald Tribune.*

Money matters

The currency in Italy is the euro. If you are coming from another country in the EU that uses the euro currency, you will not need to change money. A euro is divided into 100 cents. There are seven denominations of the euro note: €5, €10, €20, €50, €100, €200 and €500; eight denominations of coins: 1 cent, 2 cents, 5 cents, 10 cents, 20 cents, 50 cents, and €1 and €2. You can withdraw money using ATMs at many Italian banks.

Changing money

Foreign exchange counters of major banks change money.

Traveller's cheques are a safe way to carry large amounts of money when you are on holiday. Thomas Cook provides an excellent Traveller's Cheques service and offers a 24-hour refund service if they are lost or stolen (*Tel: 800 872 050*).

Credit cards

All major credit cards are accepted at most hotels, restaurants and shops in Naples. You may not be so lucky at smaller establishments.

Pharmacies

There are plenty of pharmacies (called a *farmacia*, identified by a large red or green cross) in the city centre. Chemists in the city centre with Saturday openings (rare in Naples) and who speak some English include:

Cristiano *De Tommasis, Piazza Muzi, Vomero. Tel: 081 578 3571; www.detommasis.it. Open: daily 24-hour service.*

Farmacia d'Atri *Piazza Municipio 15, Royal. Tel: 081 552 4237; www.farmaciadatri.com. Open: Mon–Sat 9am–1pm, 4–8.30pm. Closed: Aug.*

Police

The Neapolitan police force is called the *carabinieri*. Officers are very approachable; however, few speak English. The nearest police station to the city centre is the *questura centrale* (central police station) at Via Medina 75 (*Tel: 081 794 1111*).

Language

Naples may be in Italy, but the dialect is unlike that of any other part of the country. Few people speak English except in Sorrento, which is popular with British holidaymakers. Here is a list of Italian words and phrases with their English translations.

Afternoon	pomeriggio
Evening	sera
Night	notte
Hello/Goodbye	(informal) ciao
Hello	(informal) salve
Good morning	buon giorno
Good evening	buona sera
Goodnight	buona notte
Please	per favore, per piacere
Thank you	grazie
You're welcome	prego
Excuse me, sorry	mi scusi (formal), scusa (informal)
I'm sorry	mi dispiace,
I don't speak Italian	non parlo italiano
I don't/didn't understand	non capisco, non ho capito
How much is (it)?	quanto costa?, quanto viene?
Open/Closed	aperto/chiuso
Entrance/Exit	entrata/uscita
Where is?	dov'è?
Reservation, booking	una prenotazione
Breakfast/lunch/dinner	colazione/pranzo/cena
The bill	il conto
100g/300g/1kg/	un etto/tre etti/un chilo
5kg of…	cinque chili di…
A single/twin/double room	una camera singola/doppia/matrimoniale

DAYS

Monday	lunedì
Tuesday	martedì
Wednesday	mercoledì
Thursday	giovedì
Friday	venerdì
Saturday	sabato
Sunday	domenica
Today	oggi
Tomorrow	domani

TRANSPORT

Bus	autobus
Coach	pullman
Train	treno
Underground railway	metropolitana (metro)
Platform	binario
Ticket/s	biglietto/i
A ticket for…	un biglietto per…
One way	sola andata
Return	andata e ritorno
Right	destra
Left	sinistra

NUMBERS

0	zero	**5**	cinque	**10**	dieci
1	uno	**6**	sei	**20**	venti
2	due	**7**	sette	**50**	cinquanta
3	tre	**8**	otto	**100**	cento
4	quattro	**9**	nove		

COMMUNICATIONS

Phone	telefono
Email	posta elettronica
Fax	fax
Stamp/s	francobollo/i
Letter	lettera
Postcard	cartolina

Post offices

Usual opening hours for the *palazzo centrale della posta* (central post office) are Mon–Fri 8.15am–7pm, Sat 8.15am–noon. The post office is situated on the Piazza Matteotti.

Public holidays

The Italian public holidays are:

1 January *Capodanno* (New Year's Day)
6 January *La Befana* (Epiphany)
Easter Monday *Pasquetta*
25 April *Festa della Liberazione* (Liberation Day)
1 May *Festa del Lavoro* (Labour Day)
2 June *Festa della Repubblica* (Republic Day)
15 August *Ferragosto* (Feast of the Assumption)
1 November *Tuttisanti* (All Saints' Day)
8 December *L'Immacolata* (Feast of the Immaculate Conception)
25 December *Natale* (Christmas Day)
26 December *Santo Stefano* (Boxing Day)

Naples and the surrounding area also shuts down on **19 September**, the feast of the city's patron saint, San Gennaro.

Public transport

ANM buses: Routes run from 6am until roughly 11.30pm. Last buses leave the main termini of Piazza Garibaldi, Piazza Municipio and on Via Pisanelli. There is a limited nightlink service on some routes.
For further information, see www.anm.it

Metro: The new metro system is quick, clean and efficient. It's so new, there are only a limited number of stations; more are in development (due for completion in 2011). Two lines service the city centre: Metro Linea 1 and Metro Linea 6. Trains run at 5.38am– 11.52pm, depending on the line.
For information, see www.metro.na.it

Local railways: The two main overground lines you are likely to use are the Ferrovia Cumana and the Ferrovia Circumvesuviana. The Ferrovia Cumana operates services from Piazza Montesanto to Campi Flegrei (5.21am–9.41pm). The Ferrovia Circumvesuviana leaves from its own terminus in Corso Garibaldi, south of the Stazione Centrale. Trains run southeast to Pompeii, Herculaneum and Sorrento (dawn–10.30pm).
For further information, contact the train operators directly (Call centre: 7.30am–7.30pm operator; 24-hr recorded info). Ferrovia Cumana (Tel: 800 053 939; www.sepsa.it). Ferrovia Circumvesuviana (Tel: 800 053 939; www.vesuviana.it).

Religious worship

The main religion is Catholicism but there are a few synagogues and some Protestant churches.

Senior citizens

Various discounts are available for senior visitors to Naples. Travel rates and entry fees to museums and galleries are both reduced for the over 65s. You will need identification.

Student and youth travel

If you are under 18 you are entitled to reduced fares on public transport. You will need an ID card. If you are over 18 and a student, you will need a student card (for example, the International Student Identity Card).

Sustainable tourism

Thomas Cook is a strong advocate of ethical and fairly traded tourism and believes that the travel experience should be as good for the places visited as it is for the people who visit them. That's why we firmly support The Travel Foundation, a charity that develops solutions to help improve and protect holiday destinations, their environment, traditions and culture. To find out what you can do please visit *www.thetravelfoundation.org.uk*

Taxis

Three of the major taxi ranks are at the Piazza Garibaldi, Piazza Dante and Piazza Municipio. The best way to get a taxi is to phone for one: your hotel or restaurant should do this for you. Be sure only to use authorised white taxis emblazoned with the city emblem.

Taxis differ outside Naples. In Capri they are often vintage and/or convertible cars. Sorrento has horse-drawn carriages and Ischia boasts three-wheeled micro-cabs.

Telephone

Telephone numbers in the Naples area have six or seven digits with *081* as the prefix and *39* if you are dialling from abroad. Most phone booths accept phone and/or credit cards: coins are accepted in only a few locations. For directory enquiries within Italy, dial *1240*. For international enquiries, dial *176*.

Time

Italy maintains Continental European Time (GMT+1). Clocks go forward one hour in spring, and back in autumn.

Toilets

There are very few public toilet facilities in Naples. The best approach is to use the toilet in a bar. If the bar is empty it is a matter of politeness to ask the bartender first. In restaurants toilets may be for customers only.

Tourist information

The main tourist body is the Italian State Tourist Board.

For those who live in the UK, *contact the Italian State Tourist Board, 1 Princes St, London W1B 2AY. Tel: 020 7408 1254; Email: italy@italiantouristboard.co.uk; www.enit.it*

In the USA, *contact Italian Government Tourist Board, 500 North Michigan Avenue 506, Chicago, IL 60611. Tel: 312 644 0996; Email: enitich@italiantourism.com; www.italiantourism.com; or Italian Government Tourism Board, 12400 Wilshire Blvd, Suite 550, Los Angeles, CA 90025. Tel: 310 820 1898; Email: enitla@italiantourism.com; or Italian Government Tourist Board, 630*

Fifth Ave., Suite 1565, New York, NY 10111. Tel: 212 245 4822; Email: enitny@italiantourism.com

In Canada, *contact Italian Government Tourist Board, 175 Bloor St E, Suite 907-South Tower, Toronto, Ont. M4W 3R8. Tel: 416 925 4882; Email: enit.canada@on.aibn.com; www.italiantourism.com*

In Australia, *contact Italian Government Tourist Board, Level 26, 44 Market St, Sydney, NSW 2000. Email: italia@italiantourism.com.au; www.enit.it*

For more specific information on Naples, the following organisations provide tourism information.

ASST *Via San Carlo 9. Tel: 081 402 394; www.inaples.it*

Ente Provinciale del Turismo (EPT) *Piazza dei Matiri 58. Tel: 081 405 311; www.eptnapoli.info*

Osservatorio Turistico-Culturale *Piazza del Plebiscito. Tel: 081 247 1123; www.comune.napoli.it*

Travellers with disabilities

For people with disabilities Naples is a difficult city to visit. The best thing to do is to ask if someone can help. In museums and galleries the ground floors are usually accessible. Buses, however, are not wheelchair-friendly. Try using the metro and overground trains instead. New metro stations have ramps and lifts incorporated into the design. But even where ramps exist, you will often find them obstructed by cars or motorcycles.

The historic sites of Pompeii and Herculaneum, while outdoors, are little better. Access to the actual collection of ruins may have ramps, but the pathways date back to the Roman period and are littered with wheel ruts and cracks.

Weather

Naples has a Mediterranean climate with sizzling temperatures and high humidity in the summer. On the islands and coast, sea breezes make the heat more bearable.

Spring and autumn are warm and pleasant with occasional short, heavy showers. March and October are good times to visit the islands when the crowds are gone and you may see freak summer temperatures. Between November and February Naples can be bright and warm with occasional spells of cloudy weather.

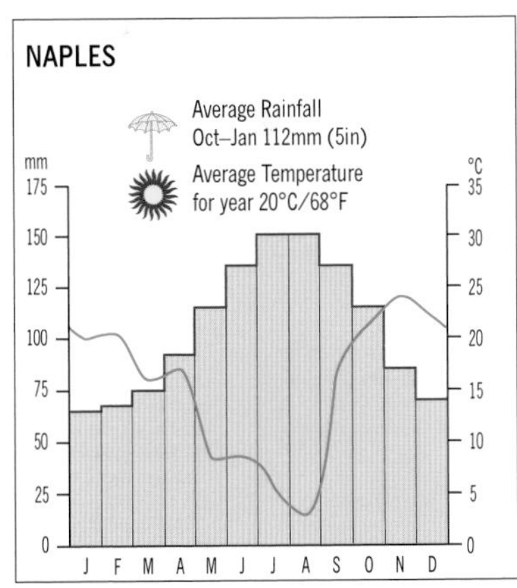

WEATHER CONVERSION CHART

25.4mm = 1 inch

°F = 1.8 × °C + 32

Index

Acknowledgements

Thomas Cook wishes to thank the photographers, picture libraries and other organisations, to whom the copyright belongs, for the photographs in this book.

BIG STOCK PHOTO 23 (Bobby Aback)
Dreamstime 80 (Razavan Cosa)
FLICKR; 25 (Kris De Curtis); 72 (Benjamin); 79 (Sean Hayford O'Leary); 98 (Flynn Wynn)
FOTOLIA 5 (Yanta)
FRANCESCO ALLEGRETTO 15, 26, 35, 43, 60, 69, 77, 113, 159, 171
MARK BASSETT 20, 38, 39, 92, 100, 117, 121, 124, 132, 137, 151, 164, 169
PICTURES COLOUR LIBRARY 1, 155
THOMAS COOK PUBLISHING 17
WIKIMEDIA 22, 67 (Lalupa); 99 (Sean William); 118 (Rolf Cosar); 73, 161 (Public Domain);
ROBERTO VUILLEMIER 139
WORLD PICTURES/PHOTOSHOT 71, 75, 91, 103, 120, 123, 165

For CAMBRIDGE PUBLISHING MANAGEMENT LTD:
Project editor: Thomas Willsher
Typesetter: Paul Queripel
Proofreader: Karolin Thomas
Index: Marie Lorimer

SEND YOUR THOUGHTS TO BOOKS@THOMASCOOK.COM

We're committed to providing the very best up-to-date information in our travel guides and constantly strive to make them as useful as they can be. You can help us to improve future editions by letting us have your feedback. If you've made a wonderful discovery on your travels that we don't already feature, if you'd like to inform us about recent changes to anything that we do include, or if you simply want to let us know your thoughts about this guidebook and how we can make it even better – we'd love to hear from you.

Send us ideas, discoveries and recommendations today and then look out for your valuable input in the next edition of this title.

Emails to the above address, or letters to traveller guides Series Editor, Thomas Cook Publishing, PO Box 227, Coningsby Road, Peterborough PE3 8SB, UK.

Please don't forget to let us know which title your feedback refers to!